Timothy Neve

Eight Sermons Preached before the University of Oxford, in the Year 1781 ..

Timothy Neve

Eight Sermons Preached before the University of Oxford, in the Year 1781 ..

ISBN/EAN: 9783337159320

Printed in Europe, USA, Canada, Australia, Japan

Cover: Foto ©Lupo / pixelio.de

More available books at **www.hansebooks.com**

SERMONS

PREACHED BEFORE THE

UNIVERSITY of OXFORD,

IN THE YEAR 1781,

AT THE LECTURE FOUNDED BY THE LATE

REV. JOHN BAMPTON, M.A.
CANON OF SALISBURY.

By TIMOTHY NEVE, D.D.
CHAPLAIN OF MERTON COLLEGE.

OXFORD:

Printed for D. PRINCE and J. COOKE, J. and J. FLECHER;
J. F. and C. RIVINGTON, and T. CADELL, *London*.

M DCC LXXX I.

TO THE REVEREND

THE VICE-CHANCELLOR

AND

HEADS OF COLLEGES;

THE FOLLOWING SERMONS,

PREACHED

AT THEIR APPOINTMENT,

ARE

RESPECTFULLY INSCRIBED

BY THEIR

OBLIGED HUMBLE SERVANT,

T. NEVE.

PREFACE.

THE following plain Discourses are sent abroad into the world merely in compliance with the injunctions of the Founder of that annual Lecture at which they were preached. With regard to the manner in which the Author of them hath discharged the trust delegated to his care, He can only say, that with more leisure and fewer avocations, his work might probably have been less faulty and better finished. But he hopes the nature of his subject is such and so important, as may atone for some defects in the execution; and that the obligation of their publication will be a sufficient apology for it.

Many attacks have been made of late, not only on some of the leading Articles of Christianity, but even on the general plan and design of it: And these have been indeed the more dangerous, from the artfulness of the mode, and from the variety and
specious-

speciousness of the colouring in which they have been delivered. Against writers of this stamp are these Discourses chiefly levelled; and perhaps there is no better method of confuting them, than by stating the truth in its genuine and scriptural light, and giving the general arguments that fair arrangement which may be necessary for those, who either cannot, or will not, examine and search diligently the whole Book of God.

The grand point which the Author has principally attempted to illustrate, is that well known but too much neglected truth, that *Jesus Christ* is the Saviour of the World, and the Redeemer of Mankind. This fundamental doctrine is first proved by the ancient Scriptures, or the argument from Prophecy; an argument, which, in its full scope and completion, is irresistible, and must convince every candid and impartial mind: But in order to induce men to judge for themselves what is right, and to search the Scriptures, whether the grand doctrines of the Christian Faith are contained

PREFACE. iii

tained therein, he has endeavoured to recommend the knowledge and study of them by some very powerful and persuasive motives. He has in the next place considered the superior desireable nature of the true knowledge of God and Christ, and the comparative excellencies of the Christian discoveries over the greatest efforts of unassisted Reason, and even the earlier Revelations of God himself under the Mosaical œconomy. These, as so many preparatory steps, tended to introduce the person and character of *Jesus the Son of God*, whose offices and high commission he hath explained, and shewed him to be every way qualified for the very important errand on which he was sent; a Light to lighten the Gentiles, that all flesh should see, and partake of the Salvation of God.

Thus was God reconciling the world unto himself: This was his gratuitous overture of Love and Mercy. It next behoves us to reflect, what part or share belongs to us, to render this so great Salvation effectual. This idea hath given occasion to an examination into the honour and reverence due to that blessed Son of God, who hath done such glorious things for us; and also hath led to an exposition of the nature and efficacy of our Christian Faith, and the necessity of the publick confession or avowal of that saving vital Faith which is the natural certain consequence of its proceeding from confirmed principles of rational conviction. But alas! as all are not Christ's that are called by his holy name: The last point, as no improper conclusion of the foregoing observations, is an inquiry into the causes and reasons why this Faith thus important and thus recommended, is not more generally and universally effectual to influence the heart and affections; and how, after all, it happens, that so many should disregard their own plain interest, and that in a matter of such essential and eternal consequence.

The Author hopes he has treated these momentous subjects with a tolerable degree of precision and accuracy; and heartily wishes his labours may be received by others, with that sincerity and good meaning with which they were written by himself.

Extract from the last Will and Testament of the late Rev. JOHN BAMPTON, *Canon of* Salisbury.

―― " I give and bequeath my Lands
" and Estates to the Chancellor, Masters,
" and Scholars of the University of Ox-
" ford for ever, to have and to hold all
" and singular the said Lands or Estates
" upon trust, and to the intents and pur-
" poses hereinafter mentioned; that is to
" say, I will and appoint, that the Vice-
" Chancellor of the University of Oxford
" for the time being shall take and receive
" all the rents, issues, and profits thereof,
" and (after all taxes, reparations, and ne-
" cessary deductions made) that he pay all
" the remainder to the endowment of eight
" Divinity Lecture Sermons, to be esta-
" blished for ever in the said University,
" and to be performed in the manner fol-
" lowing:

" I direct and appoint, that, upon the
" first Tuesday in Easter Term, a Lec-
" turer be yearly chosen by the Heads of
" Colleges

"Colleges only, and by no others, in the
"room adjoining to the Printing-House,
"between the hours of ten in the morn-
"ing and two in the afternoon, to preach
"eight Divinity Lecture Sermons, the year
"following, at St. Mary's in Oxford, be-
"tween the commencement of the last
"month in Lent Term, and the end of
"the third week in Act Term.

"Also I direct and appoint, that the
"eight Divinity Lecture Sermons shall be
"preached upon either of the following
"subjects — to confirm and establish the
"Christian Faith, and to confute all he-
"retics and schismatics — upon the divine
"authority of the Holy Scriptures—upon
"the authority of the writings of the pri-
"mitive Fathers, as to the faith and prac-
"tice of the primitive Church—upon the
"Divinity of our Lord and Saviour Jesus
"Christ—upon the Divinity of the Holy
"Ghost—upon the Articles of the Chris-
"tian Faith, as comprehended in the
"Apostles' and Nicene Creeds.

"Also I direct, that thirty copies of the
"eight Divinity Lecture Sermons shall be
"always

" always printed, within two months after
" they are preached, and one copy shall be
" given to the Chancellor of the Univer-
" sity, and one copy to the Head of every
" College, and one copy to the Mayor of
" the City of Oxford, and one copy to be
" put into the Bodleian Library; and the
" expence of printing them shall be paid
" out of the revenue of the Lands or
" Estates given for establishing the Divinity
" Lecture Sermons; and the Preacher shall
" not be paid, nor be entitled to the re-
" venue, before they are printed.

" Also I direct and appoint, that no
" person shall be qualified to preach the
" Divinity Lecture Sermons, unless he hath
" taken the Degree of Master of Arts at
" least, in one of the two Universities of
" Oxford or Cambridge; and that the
" same person shall never preach the Divi-
" nity Lecture Sermons twice."

The clear income of Mr. Bampton's estate amounts to about 120*l.* per ann.

CONTENTS.

SERMON I.

Jesus Christ the predicted Messiah.

JOHN v. 29. the last clause.
—*They are they which testify of Me.* Pag. 1

SERMON II.

The true knowledge of God and Christ.

JOHN xvii. 3.
This is life eternal, that they might know thee the only true God, and Jesus Christ, whom thou hast sent. — — 25

SERMON III.

The comparative excellency of Christian morality.

1 COR. i. 21. middle clause.
The world by wisdom knew not God. 53

SERMON IV.

Pre-eminence of the Christian over the Mosaical Law.

GAL. iii. 21. latter part.

—— If there had been a law given, which could have given life, verily righteousness should have been by the law. —— 85

SERMON V.

Time and place of birth, and the person of Christ considered.

LUKE ii. 11.

Unto you is born this day in the city of David, a Saviour, which is Christ the Lord. —— —— —— 111

SERMON VI.

Dishonouring Christ is dishonouring God.

JOHN v. 23. latter part.

—— He that honoureth not the Son, honoureth not the Father which hath sent him. 139

SERMON VII.

The neceffity of inward Faith and outward Confeffion.

ROM. x. 10.

With the heart man believeth unto Righteoufnefs, and with the mouth confeffion is made unto Salvation. ———— 173

SERMON VIII.

The caufes of the inefficacy of the Word and Faith.

HEB. iv. 2.

Unto us was the Gofpel preached, as well as unto them, but the word preached did not profit them, not being mixed with faith in them that heard it. ———— 207

Lately published by the same Author,

The comparative Blessings of Christianity, a Sermon preached before John Earl of Westmorland, Chancellor, and the University of Oxford, upon Act Sunday, July 8. 1759.

ALSO,

Animadversions upon Mr. Phillips's History of the Life of Cardinal Pole, 1766.

ERRATA.

Pag. 64. note q, l. 1. Naturas, *read* Natura—P. 71. l. 7. Teimony, *read* testimony—P. 105. l. 3. note d, Testameuto, *read* testamento—P. 143. l. 2. *after* present, *add* with him —P. 170. l. 3. from the bottom, note a, *after* one, *add* as.

SERMON I.

JOHN v. 39. the laſt clauſe.

They are they which teſtify of Me.

The whole verſe runs thus,

Search the Scriptures, for in them ye think ye have eternal life, and they are they which teſtify of Me.

IF we attentively conſider either the exalted character of the Speaker of theſe words, or the plain ſignification of the words themſelves, we cannot but look upon them as bearing a moſt important teſtimony to the grace and condeſcenſion of the Almighty, in ſupporting the ſeveral manifeſtations of his will with ſuch clear evi-

evidence of their supreme authority, that our acquiescence in, or belief of them, must manifestly appear the genuine result of rational persuasion and conviction.

To foretel future events, to point out persons hereafter to exist, and circumstantially to describe the several distinguishing peculiarities of their lives and actions, must, when the determined period arrives corresponding with the antecedent prediction, demonstrate the intervention of a superior Being, and raise the attention of the world to regard it as proceeding from *the determinate counsel and foreknowledge of him* [a], *whose word shall accomplish that which he pleaseth, and it shall prosper in the thing whereto he sends it* [b].

Viewed in this light, the assertion of our blessed Lord in the text, if understood with a view to the full scope of this argument, is a sufficient vindication of his divine mission; an ample proof that he assumed no novel or unheard of character; that he attempted no other change in the religious system of the Jews than what a long suc-

[a] *Acts* ii. 23.   [b] *If.* lv. 11.

cession

SERMON I.

cession of their own Prophets had previously and significantly marked out. Instead therefore of being looked upon by them with an evil eye, as the enemy of their Law, they ought rather to have esteemed him as the continuator and perfecter of it.

"ᶜ The Old Testament, says our Church in one of her Articles, is not contrary to the New: for both in the Old and New Testament everlasting life is offered to mankind by Christ, who is the only mediator between God and man, being both God and man." A declaration this, not only verified by that sameness of plan and design observable in each, but by the express testimony of Scripture itself. To this purpose, the author of the Epistle to the Hebrews begins his glorious defence of Christianity with this expressive position. *God, who at sundry times and in divers manners, spake in time past unto the fathers by the prophets, hath in these last days spoken unto us by his Son* ᵈ; clearly intimating, that the Christian as well as Jewish Religion owed its original to one and the

ᶜ Art. vii.   ᵈ Heb. i. 1, 2.

same

same divine Author; came equally recommended to the notice and esteem of mankind, and bore equal credentials of God's immediate inspiration: with this special difference however, that the Christian was to be introduced and established in the world at its predestined season, when it should supersede the necessity and obligation of the other.

The Gospel of Christ therefore could not be proposed to the world at its introduction, like the religion of nature, according to the scheme of modern infidels, as only fit or reasonable to be complied with, but as a matter of general and indispensable duty, enacted under the severest penalties by the authority of its divine Legislator. We cannot then wonder at the zeal and earnestness of the Apostles and first Preachers of it; or that so many should be represented as pressing into that Religion which offered the Kingdom of Heaven to its proselytes, and invited every individual to consider it as particularly addressed to himself by that God, who hath a right to command his obedience, and a power to punish his neglect or rejection of it.

And

And not more with zeal, than with sincerity and truth, did the Apostles *commend themselves*[e] and their doctrine *to every man's conscience in the sight of God:* not indeed *with the enticing words of man's wisdom*[f], by philosophical and metaphysical proofs, or abstracted reasonings; for these are not level to the capacities of the generality of mankind; but by the plainest narrations of facts done upon earth, and confirmed by miracles from heaven, evincing that *God was in them of a truth*[g], *in demonstration of the spirit and of power*[h].

Those who have attempted to maintain that strange suggestion, " that Christianity " is not founded on argument," seem to forget what hath been proved beyond all contradiction; that there are no clearer grounds and reasons, nor any of greater moral certainty, than can and have been given for the truth of the Gospel: But these, after all, have no greater weight than the force of moral evidence: This was

[e] 2 *Cor.* iv. 2. [f] 1 *Cor.* ii. 4. [g] 1 *Cor.* xiv. 25.
[h] 1 *Cor.* ii. 4.

not the apostolical method of arguing; which was a simple attestation of facts or historical truths, the testimony of which all were capable of understanding, because it was suited to the capacities of all.

The Apostles, in confirmation of what they said and what they did, were continually appealing to the written word of God, to the Law, and to the Prophets; to the Scriptures acknowledged, by those who were referred to them, to be written under the immediate direction of God's holy Spirit. Our blessed Lord himself condescended to take this method for the conviction of others of the truth of his doctrine and his mission; which appears as well from the words and reasonings of the text, as from that memorable conference with the two Disciples going to Emmaus; when *beginning at Moses, and all the Prophets, he expounded unto them in all the Scriptures, the things concerning himself* [i]. With great propriety therefore did he assure the Jews, that *had they believed Moses, they would have believed him* [k]. By appealing to

[i] Luke xxiv. 27.   [k] John v. 46.

this

SERMON I. 7

this allowed authority, St. Peter at his first Sermon converted *three thousand souls* [1] to the faith of Christ then newly risen from the dead. Thus likewise, in that noble apology which St. Paul made before Agrippa and Festus, he maintained that *he witnessed* or testified, *saying, none other things than those which the Prophets and Moses did say should come* [m]. Thus at Thessalonica, thus at Beræa, thus at Rome, *he reasoned and proved from the Scriptures, that Jesus was the Christ* [n].

It would be endless to multiply testimonies to this purpose. Such appeals as they are numerous, so are they the strongest foundation of a Christian faith. They who receive the Scriptures as the revealed will of God will be more effectually convinced by allegations derived from that decisive authority, than from all the specious principles, or refined theories, which the wit of those who are *wise in their own conceits* [o], may plausibly or needlesly invent to vindicate the ways of God to man. Such

---
[1] *Acts* ii. 14.   [m] *Acts* xxvi. 22.
[n] *Acts* xvii. 3. 11. xxviii. 23, &c.   [o] *Rom.* xii. 16.

undertakings indeed are rather superfluous. The rule is this, and it is enough: If God hath said it, it must be true; if he hath commanded it, it must be done; if he hath forbidden it, it must be avoided. These are plain and intelligible truths to all, and like first principles are so self-evident, that they admit of no dispute. Scriptural arguments are therefore the surest, the plainest, and the strongest to believers.

They who would slight such a standing Revelation, which God hath made the stated ordinary means of grace and conversion, would equally disregard a messenger, *though one rose from the dead to persuade them*[p]. Such an awful apparition might terrify and astonish them at the time, but the effects of it would be transitory, and would vanish as speedily as the spectre itself: the other would approve itself the most rational, general, and lasting means of conviction, as containing the surest evidences of our Faith, and being *able to make us wise unto Salvation*[q].

[p] *Luke* xvii. 31.   [q] *2 Tim.* iii. 15.

In

In conformity therefore to the will and direction of the liberal Founder of these exercitations, that his preachers should *confirm and establish the main articles of the Christian faith in general*[r], it surely can be no improper introduction to the succeeding discourses, to point out some of the leading or principal passages in the Old Testament, which are clear attestations of the Messiah, from his primary designation to his personal advent or manifestation in the flesh.

As the redemption, or recovery and restoration of mankind to future eternal happiness, is that gracious overture of his love which God hath communicated to us thro' the medium of the Scriptures; it may well be supposed, that sufficient intimation would be given of the means intended by God to effect it: That nothing might be wanting from time to time to strengthen the expectation, and direct the prospect of believers, in proportion to that degree of light, grace, and knowledge, which he

[r] See the Will.

vouch-

vouchsafed to bestow upon them. Without the agency of a superintending Providence, it would have been an utter impossibility to imagine, that a regular, well arranged, and consistent plan, could be carried on for upwards of four thousand years; and under the administration of different persons of various countries, callings, and interests, who, in their several successive generations, should have the same point perpetually in view; to which, as to a common center, they should all uniformly tend, without any the least variation or contradiction. Such a continued harmony and union, both of scheme and sentiment, must owe its progress as well as its rise to that God who is *great in counsel, and mighty in work*[s], *who giveth wisdom, and knowledge, and understanding*[t]. This connected plan of the divine Decrees, so visibly and regularly pursued, must, in the several stages of its advancing maturity, necessarily raise the expectation, and excite the regard of every age to that grand and momentous period, which should convincingly display the transcendent dignity of that extraordinary dispensation ordained

[s] *Jer.* xxxii. 19.   [t] *Prov.* ii. 6.

to

to be over all, and to take place in its appointed time.

Very high indeed can we trace both the neceffity and difcovery of a Mediator and Redeemer; *The feed of the woman fhall bruife the ferpent's head* [u], was the earlieft promulgation of the deftined bleffing, and was pronounced immediately after that fatal tranfgreffion of our firft progenitor, which made infirmity permanent [w]. From hence do we date, if not the rife, at leaft the firft publick intimation of Chriftianity.

This original grace and promife was fome time after renewed to Abraham, and the certainty of its accomplifhment, by repeated affurances, confirmed to him and his family. More explicit difcoveries of this intended bleffing were afterwards communicated to the patriarchs Ifaac and Jacob. To the defcendents of the latter it was more particularly limited, being reftrained to the pofterity of his fon Judah; from whom fhould proceed that great illuftrious Prophet, whom God would raife up, *and*

[u] *Gen.* iii. 15.   [w] 2 *Efdr.* iii. 22.

unto him should the gathering or obedience *of the people be*[y]. Out of the tribe bearing his name, in later times, was the regal house and family of David, in a more especial manner, selected as a type or representation of the predicted Messiah, and the state of his kingdom: the spirit of prophecy emphatically pronouncing that *the root of Jesse,* the father of the line of David, or his posterity, *shall stand for an ensign to the people; to it shall the Gentiles seek*[z], or betake themselves.

That these circumstances, so minutely prophetical of the Messiah, were eminently fulfilled in the person of our Jesus, we have every reasonable, every possible satisfaction that the argument will admit of. We have a twofold history of his pedigree respecting the succession of his natural and legal parentage, transmitted to us by two of the Evangelists, who wrote the his-

---

[y] *Gen.* xlix. 10. יקהת from יקה. Dicto audiens fuit, paruit, obedivit, so Aynsworth. In this sense the word is rendered by our translators, *Proverbs* xxx. 17. It occurs only in these two places.

[z] *Is.* xi. 10. דרש, cum præpositione אל, non significat quærere, sed tendere, confluere aut se conferre. *Deut.* xii. 5. Bootii Animadv. ad Textum Heb. Vet. Test. L. i. c. v. s. vi. p. 36.

tory

tory of his life, in the very age in which he had appeared, and within a very few years after his afcenfion.

Had the relations they give of our bleffed Lord's defcent been as falfe, or inconfiftent, as fome cavillers have taken pains to reprefent them, they would have been inftantly detected at the very time of their publication. The Jews would have objected to their report, and called the veracity of their tables in queftion. As nothing of this appears, their teftimony muft remain unimpeached. Some difficulties may feem perhaps to embarrafs both the genealogies in their prefent ftate; yet are they eafily reconcileable, and the objections of no material confequence: Both of them being full and clear in this principal point, (which indeed is all that we are required to believe concerning them, and is enough for our comfort and fatisfaction) that Jefus was of the feed of Abraham, of the family of David, and born in the flefh of the Virgin Mary [c].

[c] See this fubject very accurately confidered, in Mr. Yardley's Critical Examination and Defence of the Genealogies of Jefus Chrift, as recorded by St. *Matthew* and St. *Luke*.

So incontrovertible was this particular, that the author of the Epistle to the Hebrews appeals, in the most direct and positive terms, to the Jews themselves for the truth of it. *It is evident,* says he, *that our Lord sprang out of Judah* [d]. This fact they neither did, nor could pretend to deny. His parents, at the general taxation of the empire, had been publickly registred as being *of the house and lineage David* [e]. In a case of such high importance, and which would be so much enquired into by the Jewish people, it was absolutely incumbent upon the Evangelists to be exact and faithful in collecting and preserving the records of the origin and birth of Jesus Christ; " so as to deliver a truth, not only that " could not be gain-said; but also, that " might be proved and established from " certain and undoubted rolls of ancestors, " at that time well enough known, and laid " up in the publick repositories, and in the " private also [f]."

[d] *Heb.* vii. 14.   [e] *Luke* ii. 4.
[f] Lightfoot's Horæ Hebraicæ, &c. Vol. II. p. 96.

Those

Those persons, likewise, who were more immediately called to the prophetical function, expatiate largely in their description of his character and office, in all its several branches; delineating, with the utmost precision, the greatness and extent of those blessings to be derived from him, who, like the sun in the natural world, should *arise with healing in his wings*[g]; and be the source and fountain of religious grace and knowledge to every people, and nation, and language: It being the principal purpose of their appointment *to testify beforehand the sufferings of Christ, and the glory that should follow*[h].

The Prophet Isaiah, who, by way of eminence and distinction, is called the Evangelical Prophet, because he foretold so great a variety of events, respecting the regal and sacerdotal, the exalted and the humiliatory state of the Messiah, is very copious upon this subject. His whole book is full of the most sublime and magnificent images expressive of the grace, and

[g] Mal. iv. 2.   [h] 1 Pet. i. 11.

love,

love, and goodness of God; and of the state and the privileges, of the glory and the felicity of Christ's kingdom. He acquaints us with all the memorable circumstances attending his nativity, with the greatness of his excellency, his high original, his inherent divinity, and his preexistent state; with the value and efficacy of his sufferings, his complete satisfaction, and his meritorious intercession; with the rejection of the Jews, and with the call and acceptance of the Gentiles. These are topicks on which he dwelleth with particular ardour and energy.

This is the language of succeeding Prophets. *Living waters*, says Zechariah, *shall go out of Jerusalem; the Lord shall be king over all the earth: in that day there shall be one Lord, and his name one*[i]: Jeremiah's *righteous branch of David, the Lord Jehovah our righteousness*[k]: Ezekiel's *one king, and one shepherd of Israel*[l]: Micah's *ruler in Israel, whose goings forth have been from of old from everlasting*[m]: Haggai's *desire of all nations*[n]: Malachi's *messenger*, or angel, of

---

[i] Zach. xiv. 8, 9.   [k] Jer. xxiii. 5, 6.   [l] Ezek. xxxvii. 22. 24.   [m] Mic. v. 2.   [n] Hag. ii. 7.

the

the covenant°. These several predictions are abundantly expressive of the eternity, the divine nature, and person of the Messiah, and have been always constantly applied by the ancient Jews to the time of his appearing. To the same purpose, in like manner, Jacob's *Shiloh* ᵖ, Balaam's *star of Jacob* and *sceptre of Israel* ᵍ, Job's גאל ʳ, or rescuer from destruction and death, and the like, cannot be consistently interpreted, according to the general tenor of Scripture; if they be not considered as so many concurrent references to the person and grace, the power and kingdom of Christ. How amazingly full and particular in his predictions, and punctual in all the circumstances of them, is the Prophet Daniel in stating the precise time of Messiah's appearance; and how exactly correspondent is the narrative of the evangelical historians to the minutest transactions, ages before pronounced to be performed by him. who was to be the Messiah; so that the predictions have already received an abundant verification in their accomplishment.

° *Mal.* iii. 1. ᵖ *Gen.* xlix. 10. ᵍ *Num.* xxiv. 17.
ʳ *Job* xix. 25.

But moreover besides these direct allusions and prophecies, there were several persons, events, and things under the Jewish dispensation, intended either as emblematical representations, or prefigurative types, foreshadowing by some legal ceremony or other, the various states of the Messiah; and in their general plan tending to illustrate the grand doctrine of the mediatorial scheme. The command to *Abraham* to offer his son *Isaac*[s]; the blessing imparted to *Judah*[t]; the sufferings, exaltation, and person of *Joseph*; the priesthood of *Melchizedek* and *Aaron*; the call, election, and government of *Moses*; the triumphs of *Joshua*; the reign of *David*; the redemption of the first-born; the brazen serpent; the killing of sacrifices, more especially of the *Paschal Lamb*; the actions and ceremonies upon the great day of expiation, attending both the *scape goat*, and the *goat* appointed for the *sin offering*, whose blood was to make *atonement*[v]: All these various mystical emblems, whether

[s] *Gen.* xxii. 22. *Gen.* xlix 8—12.
[v] *Lev.* xvi.

personal,

SERMON I.

personal, occasional, or perpetual, look to one and the same grand character which gave them their importance.

Indeed the whole œconomy of the Jewish law, as the authority of Inspiration assures us, *was our Schoolmaster to bring us to Christ*[a], having a secondary and symbolical meaning, only to be illustrated by a Saviour's person, acts, and character. And though from the nature, subject, and design of the Old Testament, a literal and historical sense is manifest; yet as the several particulars were analogical to the signs and times of the Messiah, and the chief resemblances remarkably coincident in both, they may justly be deemed appropriated to him, as having their completion in the correspondent antitypes of the Christian dispensation.

The truth of this will be evident, if we advert to the general scope of the Epistle to the Hebrews; which, whilst it explains the whole system of the Gospel by proofs drawn from the Old Testament, (which

[a] *Gal.* iii. 24.

were arguments well calculated to convince that people,) is the beſt of comments upon the Levitical law: It alſo, by the cleareſt and moſt ſolid reaſoning, demonſtrates the reciprocal connection between the two Religions; that each in its reſpective adminiſtration tends to the ſame end, being only one continued harmonious illuſtration of the wiſdom, power, and goodneſs of God, exerted for the advantage of mankind; the one ſo elucidating the other, that the Law is not improperly ſtyled the Goſpel veiled, and the Goſpel the Law revealed, as its *veil was done away in Chriſt* [w]*:* that ſo from contemplating the authority, love, and counſel of God, the glory of his Son might be more conſpicuous, and that our *faith and hope* through him *might* ultimately *be* or reſt *in God* [x].

The books and prophecies of the Old Teſtament were written many centuries before the coming of Chriſt, We have received them from the profeſſed enemies to his faith: whoſe intereſt it would have

---

[w] 1 *Cor.* iii. 14. Ει Χριϛω καταγειται.
[x] 1 *Pet.* i. 21.

been,

been, either to have suppressed the truth, or to have given a different interpretation of those passages in the Old Testament, which we constantly appeal to as clear testimonies of our Jesus being the Messiah. This however they have not done. Some indeed of the later Rabbinical writers have taken a greater latitude in their expositions of those sacred volumes: yet the more ancient Jewish doctors invariably interpret those very passages, as actually prophetical of, and solely applicable to that person and character whom they still fondly expect: whose coming is even at this day, a fundamental article of their Creed, and the subject of their Prayers, and expressed frequently in those very words of Scripture which are applied in the New Testament to the Messiah [y].

In short, the sum and substance of the Scriptures is plainly this, the Revelation of Christ, or *the testimony of Jesus* [z]. He who is promised in the Old Testament, is exhi-

---

[y] See Bishop Chandler's Defence of Christianity, ch. ii. sect. i. p. 49, &c. See also Dr. Lightfoot's Works. *passim*.
[z] *Rev.* xix 10. See Bp. Hurd's Warburton's Lectures.

bited in the New as fully anfwering all the different ideas of fo publick and comprehenfive a character[a]. If the witnefs of the former be true, fo muſt the other, as being foretold by that, be alfo true; and, both confidered together, amount to a full, cogent, and fufficient atteſtation, that our bleſſed Jeſus was the perſon ſo ſpoken of before; that he came from God, and that his religion being thus evidently of Divine Appointment, muſt be the only poſſible way of Salvation.

Thus may we confidently truſt the cauſe and merits of Chriſtianity to a ſtrict and

---

[a] Totum vetus Teſtamentum Chriſtum in ſe continet, ut poſtea ab Apoſtolis eſt prædicatus. . . . Hinc diſcitur et hoc, legem et Prophetas nequaquam cognoſci, aut rite prædicari, ſi non in iis involutum Chriſtum invenias et adores. Verum quidem eſt, haud apparet in his Pannis Chriſtum eſſe involutum: quare et Judæi videre ipſum nequeunt. Contempti adeo et nulla ſpecie Panniculi ſunt, neglecta verba quæ videntur de nullius pretii verbis externis loqui, ut ſane per ſe intelligi nequeant: propterea ex Novo Teſtamento, ex Evangelio lucem inferri illis, et cognoſci ea oportet. . . . Primum ex Evangelio Chriſtum diſcere oportet: inde illico videre licet quam pulchre omnia veteris Teſtamenti ipſum reſpiciunt, et de eo teſtantur. . . . Summa hæc eſt totius divinæ Scripturæ. Lutheri Poſtillæ majores, ſeu Conciones ex evangelicis hiſtoriis defumptæ per univerſum annum. Baſileæ, 1546. fol. Concio in Feſt. Nativ. Chriſti, p. 58.

impartial

impartial examination of the Scriptures. The facts related in them were not done in a corner. The writings which preserve the memorials of them are not kept secret from public view and inspection. All men are earnestly invited to search and enquire whether these things are so or not; that from their own observation they may know and be convinced of the truth and certainty of them; and that there are the most undoubted assurances of their genuineness and authenticity. Whatsoever is produced out of these standing and inspired records of truth and antiquity, cannot but most satisfactorily confirm the credibility of the Gospel, which was from the beginning of time originally decreed to be established upon the foundation of the Jewish covenant: for *these* things *were written that we might believe that Jesus is the Christ, the Son of God*[b]; *he of whom Moses in the law, and the prophets did write*[c]; *who came not to destroy the law and the prophets, but to fulfil them*[d]; for to him do they all look, and *of him do they all testify*.

[b] *John* xx. 31.   [c] *John* i. 45.
[d] *Matt.* v. 17.

SERMON II.

JOHN xvii. 3.

This is life eternal, that they might know thee the only true God, and Jesus Christ, whom thou hast sent.

THE contemplation of the being of God, and of his goodness to mankind, as displayed in the immense variety there is in nature, and in the beauty, order, and excellency of the works of Creation. is a noble and delightful employment of the human mind. But this, glorious as it is, affords only a speculative or philosophical knowledge of God; such indeed as may convince an Atheist, but not

not satisfy the ardent desires of a Christian. To know or believe in general that there is a God, some supreme self-existent Being, who is the author of nature, who hath given life and being unto us, and to every other creature, must undoubtedly yield us no small pleasure in the discovery, from the exercise and improvement of our intellectual faculties; but can suggest to us no nearer a relation to him, than that of Creator and Governour of the universe.

But how low and imperfect will this seem, when compared with that more useful and comfortable knowledge which we learn from the Gospel; this most reviving doctrine, *God in Christ, reconciling the world unto himself*[a]; and *Christ in us, the hope of glory*[b]. This acquaints us with the near and dear relation which we bear to God; that he regards us not only as his creatures, but his children; that he looketh upon us with all the affectionate tenderness of a parent; that he hath provided all things for our well-being in this life, and fitted

[a] 2 *Cor.* v. 10. [b] *Col.* i. 27.

us for eternal happiness in a future state; that by adoption and grace he hath exalted us to the high honour of becoming his sons, and heirs of the kingdom of heaven.

The metaphysical proofs of God are difficult and intricate, and generally beyond the reach of common capacities; but the Scriptures lay before us the plainest and most amiable idea, of his being a God of infinite mercy, love, and consolation. To consider him in no higher light than as the author of nature, is next almost to the not knowing him at all: *For*, as St. Paul argues with his Roman converts, though *the invisible things of him from the creation of the world are clearly seen, being understood by the things that are made, even his eternal Power and Godhead* [c]; yet he maintains, that such knowledge is altogether insufficient for practice: Because, that when men *knew God*, or had thus traced out his footsteps by reason and philosophy, *they*, nevertheless, *glorified him not as God* [d]. Though their minds were enlightened, and their

[c] *Rom.* 1. 20. [d] *Rom.* i. 21.

understandings improved with this degree of natural knowledge; still their hearts were so darkened by polytheism and idolatry, that *they changed the glory of the incorruptible God, into an image made like to corruptible man, and to birds, and fourfooted beasts, and creeping things* [e]. What a deplorable account is this of pagan theology! serving however to convince us from fact, that such an imperfect knowledge of Religion which men derive from nature and reason, exclusive of Revelation, cannot preserve them either from the grossest idolatry and superstition, or from entertaining the lowest sentiments of the Deity. This is sufficiently apparent from the practice of all the heathen nations, which ever have been, or are still this day upon every part of the earth; who can be considered in no other religious light, than as *ignorant worshippers of an unknown God* [f].

This was the state of Religion, even in the politest and most civilized parts of the world, before the manifestation of the Son of God in the flesh. Almost, in the lite-

[e] *Rom.* i. 23.   [f] *Acts* xvii. 23.

ral sense of the words, *they had no hope, and were without God in the world* [g]; ignorant of his true nature; and paying a blind service and homage to dumb idols of wood and stone. To evince the vast disparity between Heathenism and Christianity, and the miserable condition of the former, there cannot be a stronger or more expressive idea conveyed to us, than that constant and familiar image of darkness contrasted with light; which so frequently occurs in Scripture, to denote the forlorn state of that spiritual death and wretched ignorance which universally prevailed; till *God who commanded the light to shine out of darkness, shined in our hearts, to give the light of the knowledge of the glory of God in the face* or person *of Jesus Christ* [h]; who is elsewhere described as that *true light, which, coming into the world, enlighteneth every man* [i].

---

[g] *Ephes.* ii. 12.
[h] 2 *Cor.* iv. 6.
[i] *John* i. 9. So is this verse rendered by Doddridge in his Exposition, and by Beausobre and Lenfant in their translation of the New Testament, and by Dr. Hammond: Compare *John* iii. 13. xi. 27. and xii. 46. in his Annotations.

To this celestial Light did the Scriptures of the Old Testament bear witness. To this evidence did the blessed Jesus appeal. By fulfilling ancient prophecies; by signs, and wonders, and miracles; by communicating the same astonishing powers to his Disciples, and by many other infallible proofs; it was clear, and undeniable, that he was that Redeemer, who had been so long before ordained in Heaven, revealed in Paradise, foreseen by the Patriarchs, and spoken of by all the Prophets. With such indisputable credentials of authority, *every word which proceedeth out of his mouth*[k] demands an humble and a serious attention: for *never man spake like this man*[l]. His love and the greatness of his power *to save them to the uttermost, who come unto God by him*[m], no where appear in stronger colours, than in those endearing expressions of his selected for the subject of our present meditations. *This is life eternal to know thee the only true God, and Jesus Christ, whom thou has sent,* as the great Prophet, Priest,

[k] Luke iv. 22.   [l] John vii. 46.
[m] Heb. vii. 25.

and

and King into the world, to publish *the everlasting Gospel*[n], and *to cause righteousness and praise to spring forth before all the nations*[o].

This is the great and glorious truth inculcated in the text, which we will endeavour to illustrate, by considering,

> First, The force and meaning of the words:
>
> Secondly, The doctrine contained in them:
>
> Thirdly, The desireable nature of the knowledge they instill and recommend.

The words themselves may perhaps well enough bear another construction, and by a small alteration in the punctuation, be thus rendered: This is life eternal to know thee, and Jesus Christ, whom thou hast sent, to

[n] *Rev.* xiv. 6.
[o] *Is.* lxi. 11.

be the only true God [p]. Thus making them bear their testimony to the essential, inherent divinity of the blessed Jesus and his consubstantiality and coequality with the Father: Thus was this verse understood and interpreted by some of the ancient writers of the church. In this sense they well agree with the reasoning in the context [q]. Our blessed Lord, in the course of his pathetick address to the Father, appeals to that original *glory which he had* in unity *with him,* as his eternal coessential Son, before the birth of time, or the existence of things, even *before the world was* [r]; and proclaims aloud, that *having finished the work he had given him to do* [s], and being *no more* to continue *in the world, he was coming to him* [t], to resume his pristine glory.

Taking the words however in the sense and order in which they are placed in our translation, they are eminently declaratory

---

[p] Αυτη δε εστι αιωνιος ζωη ινα γινωσκωσι σε τον μονον αληθινον θεον και ον απεστειλας Ιησουν χριστον.

[q] See Wheatly's Lady Moyer's Lectures, Sermon V. p. 250, note [B.] Novatian and S. Austin cited by him. See also Ambrosius de Fide, L. v. cap. i. Inter Opera, vol. iv. p. 183.

[r] *John* xvii. 5.   [s] *John* xvii. 4.
[t] *John* xvii. 11.

SERMON II.

of our Saviour's mediatorial powers; expresly defining life eternal to be, or to consist in the knowledge of God in Christ. Such, and so great, is *his* transcendent excellency, who is the *express image* or representation *of the person of the Deity* [u]; and who, in a peculiarly eminent manner, *could manifest his name* and will, *unto the world* [w]. The Almighty himself, from the spirituality and immensity of his essence, is an object too resplendent for human eyes to behold, or for the human understanding to comprehend. Through this appointed medium, *his Son sent in the likeness of sinful flesh* [x], hath he condescended familiarly to manifest himself to the sons of men; that so, the glories of that Supreme Being, the author of life and immortality, *who dwelleth in the light, which no man can approach unto, whom no man hath seen nor can see* [y], might be plainly discoverable in him, who is the incarnate *brightness of his glory, and the express image of his person* [z]: Hence it might truly, and

[u] *Heb.* i. 3.   [w] *John* xvii. 6.   [x] *Rom.* viii. 3.
[y] 1 *Tim.* vi. 16.   [z] *Heb.* i. 3.

C   with

with strict propriety of speech, be said of them *who had known and seen him, that they had known and seen the Father also* [a].

Our blessed Lord doth indeed in the passage before us, call God the Father, *the only true God*. Yet certainly, not with any intention to exclude himself from a right to that appellation; or to suggest any contradistinction between himself and the Father; but in direct opposition to idols, to the false and fictitious gods of the heathen world [b]. Eternal life is here affirmed to depend as much upon the knowledge of Jesus Christ, as upon the knowledge of God the Father: Both, in this respect, are spoken of, as of the same divine nature, and equal in power, dignity, and glory: the knowledge of both, as God and as Mediator, is equally necessary; the life of grace opening the way to the life of glory.

This is that saving necessary knowledge revealed to us in the gospel œconomy: and

---

[a] *John* viii. 19. and xiv. 9.
[b] Dr. Randolph's Vindication of the Doctrine of the Trinity, part ii. p. 66. Dr. Bishop's Moyer's Lectures, Sermon II. p. 54—60.

we then *know Christ*, when we attend to him as the Son of God; when, in an honest and good heart we receive the declarations he hath made of the will of his heavenly Father; and are thoroughly sensible that *there is none other name under heaven but his, whereby we must be saved*[c]. To give us the compleatest idea of the nature of this faith; it is the uniform language of Revelation, that *He only that hath the Son hath life eternal*[d]. *He shall not come into condemnation, but is passed from death unto life*[e]. With such suitable marks of love and mercy is the blessed Jesus, conjointly with the Father, recommended to us as the author of our faith, the encourager of our hopes, and the bestower of life eternal. This is the knowledge held out to us in the text.

We will now, secondly, consider more largely the Doctrine taught and contained in it.

[c] *Acts* iv. 12.   [d] *John* v. 11, 12.
[e] *John* v. 24.

The most endearing representation that can be made of the Gospel of Christ is, when it is exhibited as the display of Divine Philanthropy, offering life and pardon to as many as will answer the call. It then eminently appears *the power of God unto Salvation* [f], communicating to the world the inestimable treasures of that heavenly wisdom which terminates in the honour of God, and the benefit of mankind: A knowledge not consisting of idle speculations, but substantial virtues.

Indeed to know God as he is, and to order our conceptions aright concerning him, though an essential and primary part of Religion, is yet the peculiar gift of him, *from whom cometh every good and perfect gift* [g]. How vainly did the ancient philosophers employ themselves in the search of happiness, or the supreme good; concerning which there were almost as many opinions as men; all their enquiries ending in the same doubt and dark-

[f] *Rom.* i. 16.   [g] *Jam.* i. 17.

ness,

ness, in which they were originally involved. Whereas we Christians are made acquainted with every important truth, whether relating to God the first cause, or to his agency in second causes, upon the surest ground, and most infallible testimony, the word and spirit of God. And this is the criterion of our faith, *If any man will do his will, he shall know of the doctrine, whether it be of God*[h]. The evidence of its divine authority will readily be acknowledged by those, who compare the inward dictates of their hearts with the leading principles of their Religion.

What excellency of speech or charms of eloquence can so effectually operate upon an upright mind, as the plain persuasive oratory of the Gospel? How powerfully does it enforce upon the consciences of men, the great truths of God's high Attributes, his providence, his will, his commands, his promises, and his threatnings? Where are the arguments for the immortality of the soul, a future judgement, and

[h] *John* vii. 17.

everlasting rewards and punishments, declared with such perspicuity, credibility, and authority; so as to need no extraordinary skill, sagacity, penetration, or judgement, to understand their import, and perceive their force? *He who receiveth this testimony, will set to his seal that God is true*[i], and will fulfil his gracious promises, *that whosoever believeth in him shall not perish*, as in his natural state he certainly would do, *but have eternal life*[k].

This spiritual eternal life results from the knowledge of God and Christ, and is the blessed consequence of the Gospel Covenant; which, at its earliest dawn, was attended with such prodigious efficacy and astonishing operations, as fully attested its author and finisher to be God. In his own person he is described to be *God manifest in the flesh*[l]: " It be-
" coming him by whom all things are,
" to be the way of Salvation to all,
" that the institution and restitution of
" the world might be both wrought by

[i] *John* iii. 33.   [k] *John* iii. 15.
[l] 1 *Tim.* iii. 16.

" one

"one hand [1]." Moreover, the reformation of manners, which accompanied the manifestation of this grace, bespeaks its high original. When *the whole world lay in wickedness* [m] and idolatry, *subject to the Prince of the power of the air* [n], under the prevailing influence of the great adversary to God and man; what less than a Divine Efficacy could convince and reclaim it? What less than *the Son of God manifested*, could so effectually *destroy the works of the Devil* [o].

It is recorded of one of the greatest philosophers and strongest reasoners of heathen antiquity, that he went thrice into Sicily to convert two tyrants [p]; and each time returned without success. His arguments, though supported with all the eloquence of human wisdom and address, were not sufficient to overcome the prejudices of those two sinners. But when Peter, full of the Holy Ghost, preached in the name

---

[1] Hooker's Ecclesiastical Polity, Book V. Sect. 51.
[m] *John* v. 9.   [n] *Ephes.* ii. 2.   [o] 1 *John* iii. 8.
[p] The elder and the younger Dionysius of Syracuse. Diog. Laertius de vitis Philosophorum, vol. i. edit. Meibomii, in vit. Platonis, L. iii. segm. 18—23. et Plutarchi Vita Dionis.

of Jesus, multitudes were converted at once: and when Paul, rejecting all the superfluous ornaments of man's oratory, *came and declared the testimony of God*[q], and *the mind of Christ*[r], he not only converted the kingdom of Sicily, but almost the whole world. So widely different are the power and effect of divine and human operation, the opinions formed by the reasoning of philosophy, and the conviction wrought by the evidences of the Gospel.

Indeed, what influence could the maxims of Pagan theology well have upon the hearts of men, when it was a matter of the utmost indifference into what religious sect or party any of them were received. The philosophers in general did not attempt to enjoin their dogmas upon the cogent principles of duty and obligation. They deemed it sufficient to conform to the established Rites of their country's religious worship[s]. With a different view was the knowledge of God in Christ recommended; not to

---

[q] 1 *Cor.* ii. 1.   [r] 1 *Cor.* ii. 16.
[s] See Pythagoras's Golden Verses, *Init.* and Plato's Phædon, *circa fin.*

this

this or that individual, to this or that nation, but to every creature, to the whole world, *that the world through him might be saved*[s]. The disobedience of the first Adam had involved all his posterity, even the whole human race, in his fall and condemnation. The meritorious perfect obedience of this our second Adam, is exhibited in the Gospel, *making* as *many righteous, unto justification of life*[t]. As the fall, was universal, so was the redemption, and extended to all, *for that all have sinned*[u]: not, however, absolutely or unconditionally; for though proposed and offered to all, it is profitable only to those who hear, who receive, and who with the heart believe unto effectual justification. Such a faith welcomes Christ in all his offices; for it admits his Revelation, trusts in his Atonement, and flies to him for Righteousness and Life eternal. This is what an Apostle calls *the substance*, or confident expectation, *of things hoped for, the evidence*, or conviction, *of things not seen*[w]. On this we found our claim, our especial privilege

[s] *John* iii. 17.   [t] *Rom.* v. 18.   [w] *Heb.* xi. 1.
[u] *Rom.* v. 12.

to be called the Sons of God. By this we are entitled to those blessings, to which belong both *the promise of the life that now is, and of that which is to come* [x].

Lord, may we all say with St. Peter, *to whom shall we go, thou hast the words of eternal life* [y] : *Thy words are spirit and they are life* [z]; they guide us to, and *they sanctify us through the truth* [a]; and thereby are we delivered from the fear of evil, and the power of the evil one. The sure and happy effect of this gospel spiritual knowledge, is a chearful and unfeigned obedience to the will and commands of our Master; for *hereby do we know that we know him, if we keep his commandments* [b]. This is life eternal, or the way and means to obtain it, thus and after this manner, *to know the only true God, and Jesus Christ whom he hath sent.* This includes the whole Christian dispensation, what all must believe and do, to inherit eternal life.

[x] 1 *Tim.* iv. 8.   [y] *John* vi. 68.   [z] *John* vi. 63.
[a] *John* xvii. 20.   [b] 1 *John* ii. 3.

Thirdly,

Thirdly, Proceed we now to consider the desireable nature of this knowledge.

It is the highest and most sublime knowledge that can possibly be recommended; having the most glorious objects to contemplate, and being conversant with the most important truths. The wisdom of Solomon was so renowned as to draw admirers from distant nations to hear and to learn from him : yet the Christian Lawgiver and Teacher is infinitely wiser and greater than that accomplished Prince, though *he exceeded all the kings of the earth in wisdom* [c]. The doctrines of Christ, as taught in the Gospel, however to *perishing* sinners they may seem *foolishness* [d] ; yet are they most signal and illustrious memorials both of *the power and the wisdom of God* [e]. They contain not indeed the worldly knowledge of any science, art, or profession, invented and improved by human industry and penetration: but, in them is declared the wisdom of that Almighty Being who is only wise; who of,

[c] 1 *Kings* x. 23. [d] 2 *Cor.* i. 18.
[e] 1 *Cor.* i. 24.

and

and in himself, knoweth and seeth all things; even the knowledge of his Attributes and perfections, as far as the human mind can comprehend him; and his relation to all his creatures, more especially to us men, to whom he thus communicates the grateful intelligence of all high and heavenly mysteries.

How diligent are we to search into the histories of former ages? how eager after new discoveries, which concern us little or not at all? how fond to hear and read of distant nations and people; not so much perhaps for any proposed advantage, as to indulge a laudable desire of knowledge? Is it because we are delighted with the relation of things strange and uncommon? assuredly, there is nothing can be reported of any people or country whatsoever, that exceeds the bounds of Nature or the reach of Reason: nothing new or wonderful like those inexhaustible and unsearchable mysteries of the love and greatness, the grace and glory of Christ, whereby *we are filled with all the fulness of God*[f]. Nay, supposing all to be

[f] *Ephes.* iii. 19.

true

SERMON II.

true which we are told of the riches, power, and grandeur of the greatest princes of the world; what are they to the infinite majesty of him, who is the King of kings and the Lord of heaven and earth, and to the all-sufficient fulness of our Redeemer? Our knowledge of the former, however pleasing or ornamental, is yet circumscribed within a short period of time, and the narrow bounds of our finite shallow understandings: but the knowledge of God in Christ, reaches from the beginning of time to the endless ages of eternity; and is replete with the glad tidings of such blessings which *eye hath not seen, nor ear heard; neither hath it entered into the heart of man to* conceive *the things which God hath prepared for them that love him* [g].

Under the influence of such conviction St. Paul, though *brought up at the feet of Gamaliel, and taught according to the* best and most *perfect manner of the law* [h], a great orator, and an eminent proficient in all divine and human literature, *counted* all

[g] 1 Cor. ii. 9. [h] Acts xxii. 3.

these rare endowments, and even his national privileges, but as so much *loss*, when put in competition *with the excellency of the knowledge of Christ Jesus our Lord*[l]; which, as he elsewhere expresses it in very emphatical words, *is without controversy, the great and* incomprehensible *mystery of godliness*[k], the most important and wonderful knowledge, and what only is necessary to be sought after and acquired.

In good truth, the doctrine of Christ's Incarnation and Passion, and of his unspeakable love in our Redemption, infinitely surpasses all that can be said or thought. If this doth not challenge a submissive and anxious attention, surely nothing can. This hath been the joyous consolation of holy and pious persons in every age of the world; this is that *of which the Prophets of old enquired and searched diligently*[l]; this is *what Abraham* the father of the faithful *rejoiced to see*[m]; and not he alone, but *many kings and prophets desired*[n] the same: !yea, *the very*

[l] *Phil.* iii. 8. [k] 1 *Tim.* iii. 16. [l] 1 *Pet.* i. 10.
[m] *John* viii. 56. [n] *Luke* x. 24.

angels themselves in heaven, who enjoy the beatifick vision of God, account this knowledge of the Gospel, this love of God in Christ, as a part of their happiness; for *they desire to look into these things* º, and, with the utmost wonder and rapture, to contemplate and adore this *manifold wisdom of God* ᵖ. What a reproach will it be to us, if we should be unaffected by the love of Christ for us; if we " should not often " entertain ourselves with the delightful " admiration of him, and the redemption " he hath wrought for us. Towards this " good and necessary work, we have not " only the examples of the best of men " that have been, but we have them fel- " low-servants, and fellow-students, if that " can persuade us, that we may all study " the same lesson with the very angels, and " have the same thoughts with them ᵠ," to animate our love and devotion, and excite us to join them in their celestial hymns, saying, *blessing, and honour, and glory, and*

º 1 *Pet.* i. 12.   ᵖ *Eph.* iii. 10.

ᵠ Archbishop Leighton's Devotional Commentary upon the first Epistle of St. *Peter*, ch. i. ver. 12. vol. i. p. 118. the last Edinburgh edition, 1748.

power,

power, be unto him that sitteth upon the throne, and unto the Lamb, that was slain, for ever and ever [r].

If this be the eucharistical chant of angels and glorified spirits, what better employment can we have upon earth, than to make that frequently the subject of our meditations, which is to be hereafter our everlasting song of praise; that with those blessed and exalted beings *we may be enabled to comprehend the breadth, and length, and depth, and height, and to know,* as far as human infirmity will admit, *that* affectionate *love of Christ which passeth knowledge* [s], which exceedeth our most elevated conceptions. What sublimity of doctrine, what excellency of wisdom, what labour of love, are apparent in the mysterious articles of our redemption! It carries us back, upon the most infallible grounds, to our creation in a state of innocency; it acquaints us with our fall, it assures us of our recovery, and gives us the promise of *an inheritance, incorruptible, and undefiled,*

[r] *Rev.* v. 12, 13. [s] *Ephes.* iii. 18, 19.

and

and which fadeth not away, being reserved in heaven for us[t]*:* shewing us in one view, what we were, what we are, and what we may hope to be hereafter. The wisest sages of the Gentile world were utterly ignorant of these wonderful particulars: having no conception of the state from whence they had fallen, they could have no apprehension of any remedy adapted to restore them to their primitive perfection.

How have the wise and learned of this world continually involved themselves in contentions and disputes concerning the very principles of natural things? With how much labour and study did one great Philosopher find out this untruth, that the world is eternal? How fond were the learned and polite Athenians of this ridiculous conceit, that they were the original offspring of their own soil, and that they sprang, like plants and trees out of the earth, by some fortuitous concurrence, they knew not what?[v] How far more consonant to the dictates of

[t] 1 Pet. i. 4.
[v] Ipsa ex sese suos cives genuisse dicitur, et eorum eadem terra parens, altrix, patria dicitur. Cicero. Orat. pro L. Flacco.

Reason and the voice of Wisdom is that doctrine of Revelation, which teacheth us, that *in the beginning God created the heaven and the earth*ᵘ: That he *formed man out of the dust of the ground, and breathed into his nostrils the breath of life, and man became a living soul*ʷ? Thus we trace our origin and descent, and are all the sons of Adam, *who was the son of God*ˣ. If the study of antiquity can delight us, here is the genuine account of the primæval source of things, before which there is nothing, but he who formed all things, and is himself *the ancient of days*ʸ. And the same Divine Authority, that thus acquaints us with the beginning of all things, informs us also, that *in the beginning*, or before all things, *the word was with God, and was God*; that *all things were made by him*; that *in him was life, and the life was the light of men*ᶻ. In so eminent a manner is distinguished the antiquity of this *knowledge of the only true God, and of Jesus Christ whom he hath sent.*

But as the most powerful incentive to the desire of this heavenly knowledge, we may

---

ᵘ *Gen.* i. 1.   ʷ *Gen.* ii. 7.   ˣ *Luke* iii. 38.
ʸ *Dan.* vii. 9.   ᶻ *John* i. 1—4.

reflect,

reflect, that even in our present state of weakness and imperfection, it supplies us with the best and most lasting comfort and delight; not only from the assurance of the pardon of our sins, but from the pleasing prospect of glory and immortality. This it was which gave the Apostles and first Christians such exceeding joy and hope in believing, and such invincible courage in suffering. The same animating and well-grounded confidence will also support us under our respective trials; will make us innocent and chearful in our lives; will take off the sting and terror of death; will give us the most solid joy in believing; and, in the end, will *minister an entrance unto us abundantly, into the everlasting kingdom of our Lord and Saviour Jesus Christ* [a].

[a] *2 Pet.* i. 11.

SERMON III.

1 Cor. i. 21. middle clause.

The world by wisdom knew not God.

The whole verse runs thus,

For after that in the wisdom of God, the world by wisdom knew not God, it pleased God, by the foolishness of preaching, to save them that believe [a].

THE Gospel of Christ can never appear in a more advantageous and interesting light, than when contrasted with

---

[a] The translators of this passage have scrupulously retained the order of the original words, and thereby occasioned a perplexity; which will soon vanish, if we rectify that inversion

the efforts of the moſt illuſtrious ſages of the heathen world to inveſtigate religious truths: the little progreſs they made in their reſearches, is a convincing proof of the natural impotency of man, to *ſearch out God*, or to *find out the Almighty unto perfection*[b]. The errors and abſurdities of their theological diſquiſitions, were, in a great meaſure, the unavoidable conſequence of their preſuming to ſpeculate upon thoſe ſubjects, which neither their acuteſt penetration could explore, nor their moſt enlarged underſtandings comprehend: Yet there abounded among them perſons of the moſt exalted genius, and moſt refined abilities, who occaſionally valued themſelves in exerting their beſt talents for the inſtruction of mankind.

ſion of the phraſe, (ſo familiar to the learned languages, but ſo unuſual in our own) and render the words, not as they are placed, but as they ought to be conſtrued. Επειδη γαρ εν τη σοφια τε θεε εκ εγνω ο κοσμος δια της σοφιας τον θεον. "*After that the world, by wiſdom, knew not God in the wiſdom of God, it pleaſed God*, &c." That is, when men with all their wiſdom could not diſcover God in his works, thoſe evident marks of his wiſdom, he revealed himſelf to them by his word.

[b] *Job.* xi. 7.

SERMON III.

St. Paul, who at his conversion was particularly commissioned to preach the Gospel *to the Gentiles*[c], was well aware of their high pretensions to wisdom and knowledge, and therefore neglected no opportunity to prove and expose the insufficiency of their several attempts at religious reformation. He lays it down, as an infallible rule, that *the things of God knoweth no man, but as he receives them* from *the spirit of God*[d], the real illuminator of the mind. He is ever magnifying the grace of Christ, and, by a variety of arguments and illustrations, labouring to convince them, that all the idolatry, superstition, and depravity of manners, which their own moralists candidly acknowledged, as too predominant amongst them, were entirely owing to their utter ignorance of the nature of God, and the spirituality of his worship. To state these matters fully and clearly, he took great pains to explain the several foundations upon which reason and faith were builded; the one requiring proof, argument, and

[c] *Acts* xxvi. 17.   [d] 1 *Cor.* ii. 11, 12.

demonstration; the other, appealing to the evidence of a divine, supernatural, and incontrovertible authority, even the testimony of God himself. To receive this testimony is faith; to know its Divine Authority, is the work of reason, in perceiving the clearness, and judging of the facts and circumstances of the evidence.

The Saviour of the world hath most expressly assured us, that *this is life eternal, that men might know the Father, the only true God, and Jesus Christ whom he hath sent*[e]. This is that divine and spiritual wisdom taught and enforced only in the schools of the Prophets and Apostles; those *holy men of God, who spake,* and wrote, *as they were moved by the Holy Ghost*[f]. This kind of knowledge therefore is the proper subject of religious faith; and, as such, demands the submission of the understanding.

Such however is the arrogance and perverseness of fallible men, the proud boas-

[e] *John* xvii. 3.   [f] 2 *Pet.* i. 21.

ters

ters of wisdom and science, that they frequently raise doubts and objections even in the plainest articles of religious truth. Hence, some have not scrupled so preposterously to magnify the powers of the human mind, as to seem well disposed to put it upon a level almost with the revealed will of God, and to set up the obscure and imperfect light of human reason, in competition with the superior advantages of Divine Grace. Hence the Scriptures have been depreciated to make room for the wild conjectures of heathen philosophy; as if human wisdom could direct us, by as near and sure a way, to happiness and life eternal, as what God himself hath pointed out in his word. Hence also, so many ingenious romances have been published in support of, what the writers have been pleased to style, the Religion of Nature, the more to extol that, and to degrade the blessings of the Gospel: This, they would insinuate, hath no pre-eminence as a rule of life; and reflect not, it is from their knowledge of Christian graces, that they so clearly see the nature and obligation

gation of that morality which they so affect to admire.

St. Paul, whose eminent abilities remarkably distinguished him; and whose mission carried him to persons of the highest rank, and to places famous for the encouragement of arts and sciences, had frequent occasions to debate this point. When engaged with the philosophers and the great men of Greece and Rome, with all the arts of a polished address, he produced a variety of arguments peculiarly calculated to raise their attention, by reasoning upon subjects immediately connected with their wisdom and philosophy. And at length declared to them, that by persevering in such *vain deceits, after the traditions of men* [g]; by their idolatry and polytheism, *they had, in reality, changed the truth of God into a lye*; for they worshipped *and served* those *creatures* [h], *which by nature are no gods* [i].

Convinced of this himself, he was anxiously solicitous to guard all his converts

[g] *Col.* ii. 8.
[h] *Rom.* i. 25.
[i] *Gal.* iv. 8.

against being seduced from the faith by *the enticing words* of *such men's wisdom*[k]; lest they should be *spoiled*, or made a prey of, by reverting to *the rudiments*, or elements, *of worldly*[l] wisdom and science. This wisdom, he expresly tells the *Corinthians* in the words of the text, is no better than so much *foolishness*; as, by a partial attachment to the gaudy colourings of a verbal oratory, the plain engaging simplicity of *the cross of Christ* would be deprived of its peculiar glory, and thereby *be made of none effect*[m]. *Where*, says he, *is the wise? where is the scribe? where is the disputer of this world?* hath not God made *foolish*, or mad the *wisdom of this world*[n]; by establishing such a scheme of Salvation which their learning and philosophy could never have thought of? Nay, though the being and wisdom of God were evident, from the works of Creation and Providence, yet *the world by wisdom knew not God.* All the powers of nature and reason, improved to their utmost perfection, could never attain to the true knowledge of the Deity, or lead men to

[k] 1 Cor. ii. 4.   [l] Col. ii. 8.   [m] 1 Cor. i. 17.
[n] 1 Cor. i. 20. Εμωρανεν.

glorify

glorify him as such; as the author and object of eternal life. But it pleased God to remove all these obstacles, and to call them by that which those sages termed, *the foolishness of preaching*; for such it seemed to them, as their pride would not permit them to enquire, and therefore they could not understand, how he, who appeared as a man, could be the Son of God; or how he, who did die, could be the author of life: though these important facts contained in them the greatest miracle of Divine Power, the greatest mystery of Divine Wisdom and Love.

From this view of things is exhibited the manifest difference there is between true and false Religion; that which we learn from nature and philosophy, and that which is *after Christ*°; the one leading to error, the other the declaration of truth. Though this point was touched upon in the preceding Discourse, yet it is worthy of a more minute and distinct enquiry. We will therefore now more particularly

° *Col.* ii. 8.

consider

consider the comparative excellency of Christian graces, with their correspondent virtues, as inculcated upon the principles of Natural Religion.

It hath already been considered how vain and uncertain the surmises of the ancient heathens were, when they sought after the knowledge of God by the mere light of nature. They had no idea, because they had no principles to argue from, of those mysterious articles, which Revelation hath discovered: of the doctrines of the Trinity, of the vicarious satisfaction of Christ, of his preternatural incarnation, of his meritorious death and passion; these and the like they could scarce have any conception of. The same also is observable of the doctrine of the resurrection of the dead; the assertion of which exposed our Apostle to the derision *of the Epicureans and Stoicks*[p]; the most learned, and, if there could be any Religion, where there was so much ignorance of God, the most religious of all the philosophers. Nay, so far were

[p] *Acts* xvii. 18.

they

they from acquiring any true knowledge, even of themselves and of the end of their creation, that, after all their most elaborate enquiries, they were not able to discover wherein their own happiness consisted. Their morality was wholly confined to outward actions; they did not, so much as in theory, understand what was the true perfection of virtue. But when they attempted to treat of the nature of the Deity, of his unity, of the soul of man, of heaven or hell, or, in their own language, of the infernal regions, or of a future state; here their boasted science ended in fancy, or wish, or at best in probability. So vain is the expectation of gathering the fruit of true wisdom, where it was neither sown nor planted.

Let us however come nearer to the point, and view those virtues and graces which, as men, we are bound to have, and to exert towards God and towards our neighbour.—In these particulars it may perhaps seem dubious at first sight, whether Christianity hath any advantage over heathenism; or whether the philosophers have

have not given as good moral lessons and rules of life, as Christ and his Apostles. Who is not almost persuaded, that they have written sufficiently about moral obligation, and well enough defined the boundaries of virtue and vice? Who also hath not heard of the patience of Socrates, the justice of Aristides, the integrity of Cato, the moderation of Scipio, and the clemency of Cæsar? It would be endless to recite examples of the very many illustrious men, who exhibited striking proofs of rare and extraordinary virtues. But, if the light of nature, nurtured by philosophy, be thus able to make men virtuous; shall we therefore take upon us to ask, what need is there so greatly to magnify Christian graces, when heathen precepts may, if attended to, have equal influence? If so, it should seem, that the supposed ascendency of the Gospel ariseth more from the prejudices of education, and the authority of teachers, than from the truth of the matter itself; and is grounded more upon partiality and opinion, than knowledge and argument.

To

To little effect indeed is the Gospel of Christ recommended as the Revelation of the most high God, if the fancies and errors of men may be brought in competition with it, and any frivolous allegations be imagined able to impair its credit.

It hath been already observed, that in those duties which immediately concern the Deity, philosophy cannot, in any degree, bear a comparison with Gospel Theology. If moreover we contemplate those intellectual virtues, which perfect the understanding, who seeth not, that the knowledge of God is the most principal, in which human wisdom, having taken great pains, hath found little success [q]? And in a more particular manner, with regard to the affections of love, fear, honour, and the like, and the actions whereby they are to be expressed, which is properly the worship of God, how blind, how profane, or ra-

---

[q] Pro comperto aliquid affirmare, aut de Dei naturas aut de ejus voluntate, solo ductu humanæ rationis, quam sit intutum ac fallax, docent tot dissonantia, non scholarum modo inter se, sed et singulorum philosophorum placita.
     Grotius de Veritate C. R. L. iii. C. 12.

ther how impious, were the speculations of philosophers. Or if a few amongst them, endowed with superior mental powers, had haply attained to some lively persuasion of the being of God, his unity and spirituality: yet how shamefully, absurdly, and wickedly did they join at the same time in the worship of a rabble [k] of Gods and Goddesses, against the light of conviction, and the testimony of their own consciences. So unable was natural reason to form a model of Religion, pure from the stains of vice, profaneness, and idolatry:—whereas, according to the Christian system, Religion is the mother and mistress of all virtues. Nay, who is there among Christians so void of honesty, so careless of his reputation, who would not disdain to be, or to be thought such as the very gods of the heathens are reported and described to have been, which yet those great men

---

[r] Quamobrem major cœlitum populus etiam quam Hominum intelligi potest, cum singuli quoque ex semet ipsis totidem Deos faciant.—Of such Deities, well might he observe, ne Deum quidem posse omnia. Namque nec sibi potestmortem conscisceie si velit . . . nec mortales æternitate donare, aut revocare defunctos, &c. Plin. Nat. Hist. L. ii. C. 7. See also Cicero de N. D. Lib. iii.

themselves scrupled not to revere as the objects of publick adoration?

That the argument however may seem not to be supported more by authority than by reason; let us try the utmost stretch of human wisdom in moral virtues, respecting the exercise of social and relative duties from man to man. The generality of the heathens had little or no other notion of happiness, but to live with as much ease, plenty and delight, as they could; to which, if a certain degree of vain glory be added, we have the sum total of all they either imagined or desired. Relative duties, enforced by no better motives, must needs want their proper support; and it was little to be expected, that those men would be scrupulously virtuous in their behaviour to others, who had so little regard to their own private virtues. Their principles, in fact were very corrupt, and their practices in consequence alike infamous; insomuch that *God gave them up*, as the Apostle observes to the Romans, *to uncleanness, to vile affections*[s], and to such filthy

[s] *Rom.* i. 24. 26.

vices as are unseemly to speak of. This was notoriously the case over all the Gentile world; and was palliated by custom and prescription both with the learned and the vulgar. Surely the knowledge of God, and the practice of moral virtues, must in vain be sought after amongst such sinners.

There are two virtues above the rest, which in our daily intercourse and converse with the world, we have frequent occasion to exercise, Justice, and Fortitude: upon these the Philosophers have descanted nobly, and have given such rules concerning them, as have done honour to themselves and to human nature. But, so far is this from detracting from the superior excellency of Christianity, that it is a confirmation of its merit: It shews, that what our Blessed Saviour taught is agreeable to the more exalted, rectified understandings of men of the most enlightened capacities; that it falls in with the powers of natural conscience, and adds new life and vigour to it. If however this plea in their behalf be thoroughly examined, we shall soon see how much they fall short of the perfection of Christian morality in those common Virtues which are confessedly their fort.

The highest pitch of justice in the school of gentile Ethicks was this rule, not to do to others, what we would not have done to ourselves. A noble maxim this for philosophy to give, and no mean attainment to arrive at this knowledge; especially if in this negative precept, the positive part be implied, which is particularly enjoined to us Christians. *Whatsoever ye would that men should do unto you, do ye even so to them*[t], is our general direction. The heathen precept is calculated solely to prevent our doing hurt: the Christian commandment is to do all the good in our power; nay, to return good for evil, even to our enemies; and in those instances also wherein we have suffered by them.

The light of reason does indeed forbid us to do evil by injustice; the light of grace exhorts us to do good from the principles of duty. He who doeth no injury, is deemed virtuous by philosophy: but, by

[t] *Matt.* vii. 12.

SERMON III.

our divine law, he who forbears to do another the same kindness he would wish to receive himself, is a sinner. As much then as doing virtuously is superior to doing nothing, so much more refined and excellent is the Christian˙ precept of justice, than the heathen notion of it.

To evince this, let us consider what one of the best and wisest of the gentile Philosophers advances upon this subject in his celebrated Book of Offices; a laboured systematical performance, which is universally allowed to be the best of its kind, and the greatest effort of human wisdom, and compare it with our theology. The first duty, says this great Reasoner, of justice is, that no man hurt another, except he be provoked by an injury [u]. Is this a doctrine fit to be named with the Christian law? Shall he presume to direct us in our duty to one another, who allows us the liberty of revenge, when irritated by an injury? What a more sublime and generous lesson doth our master dictate to us, *Love your enemies, bless*

---

[u] Justitiæ primum munus est, ut ne cui quis noceat, nisi lacessitus injuria. Cicero de Offic. L. i. C. 7.

them

them that curse you, do good to them that hate you, and pray for them which despitefully use you, and persecute you [w]. We are excited to the performance of this amiable disinterested virtue, from the view of God's universal benignity, and our relation to, and resemblance of him, when we cultivate so godlike a principle; when we thus *overcome evil with good*[x], and abhor and suppress every vindictive tendency.

If we consider the other capital virtue of fortitude; the highest elevation of it amounted only to repelling an injury [y], and testifying a stoical insensibility and contempt of death [z]; though not, at the same time, without shuddering at the terrors of it [a]. But what innumerable testimonies

---

[w] *Matt.* v. 44.   [x] *Rom.* xii. 21.

[y] Fortes et magnanimi sunt habendi, non qui faciunt, sed qui propulsant injuriam. Cicero de Offic. L. i. S. 19.

[z] Appellata est enim a viro virtus, viri autem propria maxime est fortitudo, cujus munera duo sunt maxima, mortis dolorisque contemptio. Tuscul. Quæst. L. ii. S. 17.

[a] Here all their heroism failed them. It was *so like taking a leap in the dark,* that it is no wonder if they who reckoned themselves most worthy of life, should testify the greatest indignation, when they found themselves likely soon to be deprived of it and all its blessings; for they looked not into futurity. The Grecian moralist scruples not to say, Ει δη τοιυτον εςι και το περι την ανδριαν, ο μεν θανατ⊙ και τα τραυ-
μαςα

SERMON III. 71

can Christianity produce of saints, martyrs, and confessors, of every age and sex, infinitely surpassing the reports of heathen histories; and amply expressive of that patience, magnanimity, and joy which they manifested in their trials and sufferings *for the word of God, and for the teimony of Jesus* [b].

Cato is highly and repeatedly extolled, by the same great author above referred to, for his fortitude in being his own executioner [c]. But surely the desperate exit of that celebrated person, so renowned for his

---

ματα λυπηρα τω ανδρειω και ακοντι εςαι. υπομενει δε αυτα, οτι καλον, η οτι αισχρον, το μη. και οσω αν μαλλον την αρετην εχη πασαν, και ευδαιμονιςερ۞ η, μαλλον επι τω θανατω λυποιται. τω τοιυτο γαρ μαλιςα ζην αξιον, και 8τ۞ μεγιςων αγαθων αποςερειται ειδως. v. Aristotelis Ethic. Nicom. L. iii. C. 9. A few chapters before he had mentioned death as the object of the greatest terror, because it was the conclusion or end of all things. L. iii. C. 6. Indeed, he could not well consider it in any other light; having in his first book, after much logical debate, concluded the chief good of man to consist only of things connected with the happiness and enjoyments of this present life.

[b] *Rev.* vi. 9.

[c] Cato autem sic abiit e vita, ut causam moriundi nactum se esse gauderet. Vetat enim dominans ille in nobis Deus injussu hinc nos suo demigrare: cum vero causam justam Deus ipse dederit .... tanquam a magistratu aut ab aliqua potestate legitima, sic a Deo evocatus atque emissus exierit.
Tuscul. Quæst. L. i. S. 30.

E 4 austere

auftere inflexibility, ought rather to be afcribed to fear and weaknefs, than to real fortitude of mind [d]. Had he poffeffed the true fpirit of heroical refolution, he would have triumphed over the malice of a conquering enemy. He would have defpifed that power, whofe rage and tyranny he fo greatly apprehended, as to lay violent hands upon himfelf; that he might cowardly fly from it, and avoid the mortification of being obliged to the clemency of his adverfary, for the prefervation of his life.

In the next place, let us carry on the comparifon farther, and attend to the motives, influence, and efficacy of religious principles. Here the fuperiority of the Gofpel will appear to great advantage; as its views exceed thofe of human wifdom, not only in difcerning what true virtue is, but in effecting a virtuous obe-

---

[d] Ille eas quæ nunc funt, et futura viderit, et ne fierent, contenderit, et, facta ne videret, vitam reliquerit.
Ep. ad Atticum, L. xii. Ep. 4.

Hæc differentia naturarum tantam habet vim, ut nonnunquam mortem fibi ipfe confcifcere alius debeat, alius in eadem caufa non debeat.... Catoni autem cum incredibilem tribuiffet natura gravitatem, eamque ipfe perpetua conftantia roboraviffet, femperque in propofito fufceptoque confilio permanfiffet, moriendum potius, quam tyranni vultus adfpiciendus fuit. De Offic. L. i. S. 31.

dience.

dience. True it is, that some amongst us may have so high a veneration for the writings of the pagan moralists, as to be able to select from the mass some shining fragments, and to display them with uncommon triumph and ostentation, as sufficiently powerful and persuasive to the love and practice of virtue, so as to render other inducements absolutely needless.

But in moral duty and obligation, we must attend to the matter itself, more than to the force of oratory or laboured rhetorick, as the strongest means of persuasion; and besides the duty recommended must be either necessary, suitable, or convenient. In this respect, how much more forcible must Christian motives be, than those of nature. If authority can influence, what are men to God? Wise men, supposing them such to wisdom itself? If evidence of truth be looked for, the same points have the same proofs in one, as in the other, with the peculiar confirmation of certainty in the word of God: An irresistible argument this, which philosophy was ignorant of, and could not pretend to. The best of the ancient sages were but men,
their

their writings only the compositions of men, reasoning from presumption and probability, not from assurance and demonstration; whereas the Revelation of God must be true: It commands, as well as teaches: It hath the sanction and obligation of an eternal and immutable law, which the other hath not and wants.

What moreover is the ground upon which human Wisdom forms her exhortations to Virtue? and what are the motives to support it? Chiefly this, that Virtue was to be desired for its own sake, and was its own reward. A slippery ground indeed, where even strong men could hardly keep their footing, and the rest were sure to fall[d]. It is almost next to an impossibility to persuade him, who looketh for happiness only in this life, where sense too commonly warps the judgement, that virtue is feli-

---

[e] Hæc causa est, cur præceptis eorum nullus obtemperet; quoniam aut ad vitia erudiunt, si voluptatem defendunt; aut si virtutem asserunt; neque peccato Pœnam minantur, nisi solius turpitudinis; neque virtute ullum præmium pollicentur, nisi solius honestatis, et Laudis; cum dicant, non propter aliud, sed propter seipsam expetendam esse virtutem.
L. C. Lactantius, L. iii. S. 27.

city; since daily experience must convince him of the contrary. Upon how much better a foundation do we Christians build our hopes of happiness, even upon the veracity of *God who cannot lye*[e]; and in consequence thereof upon his goodness, which hath been by the clearest demonstration evinced to us in Christ Jesus. In gospel language, holiness or righteousness is called, in one word, obedience; sin or vice, disobedience. Hence do we learn, that virtue (or godliness, as Revelation calls it) is to be desired and followed, because commanded by God, who best knows what is right and true: and as we and all things else received our being from his will and appointment, what he commands must be good and just, and his will must be the rule of goodness to all his creatures. This is that eternal foundation which cannot be shaken; this the rock upon which Christ hath builded his Church so firm, that it cannot be overthrown.

The chief arguments amongst the heathens to enforce the love and practice of

[e] *Tit.* i. 2.

virtue

virtue sprang from this principle, the hope of glory among men after their decease, or a posthumous reputation, which they dignified with the pompous name of immortality. Hence one of their gravest writers hesitates not to affirm, that there would be nothing left to encourage worthy men to virtuous actions, if we take away the reward of praise and glory [f]. Though this same philosopher wrote a treatise to prove, that virtue alone is sufficient to make men happy [g]. And yet this very virtue which was thus to confer all this felicity, he did not deem to be the gift of God, but a personal acquisition [h].

---

[f] Nullam enim virtus aliam mercedem laborum, periculorumque desiderat, præter hanc laudis, et gloriæ.
      Cicero. Orat. pro Archia Poeta, S. 11.
The same reflection occurs in the fifth Philippick; and in a fragment preserved by Lactantius he expresses himself in these words· Vult plane virtus honorem; nec est virtutis ulla alia merces. Lactantius, L. v. S. 18.

[g] Tuscul. Disput. L. v.

[h] Virtutem nemo unquam acceptam Deo retulit. Nimirum recte: propter virtutem enim jure laudamur, et in virtute recte gloriamur: quod non contingeret, si id donum a Deo, non a nobis haberemus ... Num quis, quod bonus vir esset, gratias Diis egit unquam? at quod dives, quod honoratus, quod incolumis, jovemque optimum, maximum, ob eas res appellant, non quod nos justos, temperatos sapientes efficiat, sed quod salvos, incolumes, opulentos, copiosos .... Judicium

SERMON III.

Alas! what a strange kind of immortality was that, which depended upon a breath of air, and the applause of a capricious multitude, without any other view, than to have a name recorded in the annals of history. The hopes of a future state could have no weight with men of this class: They knew not what it meant. The love of fame, not the desire of happiness, was their ruling passion. Not but that fear of punishment was as much the check, as this lust of renown was the spur to their outward actions. Poor incentives these to real inward virtue, which is neither to be enforced by terror like a slave, nor allured by the wages of an hireling.

With nobler views doth Gospel Theology, which is morality exalted, persuade Men. To know by express Revelation, that *godliness hath the promise of the life that*

---

cium hoc omnium mortalium est, fortunam a Deo petendam, a seipso sumendam esse sapientiam.
De Nat. Deorum, L. iii. S. 36.
What a falling off is here, from the grand and elevated sentiments delivered in *Sect.* 66. *Book* ii. of the same work.

now

now is, and of that which is to come[i], is the utmost that wise and good men could wish for, to direct and animate them in the pursuit and practice of Religion. Can we think, that virtue when alone is more lovely and desireable, than when the assurance of God's love and favour is superadded to the pleasing consciousness of having done our duty? Though it may be possible to attain to such refinement in speculation, as to disregard present advantages; yet who can be supposed so negligent and unwise, as to despise that perfection of virtues which unquestionably leadeth to everlasting life?

Some indeed of the brightest characters of antiquity pushed their enquiries so far as to arrive at some confused notion of the immateriality of the soul, but mixed with so much uncertainty and error, and spoken of with so much doubt and diffidence, that it may well be questioned whether they really believed it or no[k]. Some

---

[i] 1 *Tim.* iv. 8.
[k] See Dr. Randolph's Sermon upon *Rom.* i. 20. entitled, The Use of Reason in Matters of Religion, p. 24.

imagined

imagined human souls to be particles of the Deity, or anima mundi; that as such they might have pre-existed in an unknown separate state; and might, as probably, exist after the dissolution of the Body. Others supposed a transmigration of them from one body to another; and that they went to some fortunate islands or elysian fields during their state of separation from the Body. With such extravagant and chimerical reveries did they amuse themselves; betraying utter ignorance of the subject in question, and that all which they said, was mere fiction and groundless conjecture.

But whatever imaginary notions they might entertain of a future state, it was only the supposition of the soul's separate existence. They had not the least thought or apprehension of the immortality of the body by a resurrection from the dead. Here the voice of natural Religion was totally silent. Indeed some elevated minds, in their philosophical retreats, went so far as to imagine the body might perhaps be nothing more than the shell or covering, not the man himself. Sometimes they called it the

the prison, sometimes the grave of the soul; which never could enjoy its full and perfect liberty, till it had shaken off its mortal perishable part. These were but the guesses of a few: Had they been favoured with our light and certainty, how would they have exulted in the glorious hope, that both body and soul, would hereafter be united and purified in a state of complete and endless bliss.

This is the knowledge which the Gospel alone can discover: this is the comfort it offers to us, from the supreme authority and pleasure of the Almighty; from him cometh our wisdom and truth, our knowledge and certainty. Whereas the light of nature being grounded upon human wisdom and reason corrupted and depraved; can only speak of such great articles by weak arguments, and often from uncertain likelihoods concludes certain untruths. Such and so great is the difference between the wisdom of God and the wisdom of man. From the former, we have all that the saving knowledge of divine Revelation can impart: from the latter, only what the imperfect

perfect surmises of uninformed opinion can suggest, without any authority to support such random suppositions.

By the comparison in these few particulars here attempted, the superior excellency of the Gospel State is clear and manifest. We cannot but acknowledge, that no precepts of philosophy can so instruct us, no examples of history so move us, no sweetness of numbers so allure us, no force of eloquence so persuade us to godliness or virtue, as the motives, evidence, and authority of the revealed will of God. So great and powerful is the wisdom of God, so weak and unavailing the wisdom of man's reason.

Thus doth God *destroy the wisdom of the wise, and bring to nothing the understanding of the prudent* [1]. But notwithstanding this demonstration of the spirit, and power, and wisdom of God, there are those who obstinately resist such evidence. *The natural man receiveth not the things of the Spirit of God: for they are foolishness unto him; neither can he know them,*

[1] 1 *Cor.* i. 19.

because

because they are spiritually discerned[m]. They are not proved from principles of natural knowledge, which is the only wisdom he admires. Such human reasoners did from the beginning, such do still reject and oppose the Gospel; while the charms of the *wisdom of words*[n], and the arts of eloquence are abused to deprive us of our consolation, and to rob us of our reward in Christ[o]. They may indeed pretend great matters, to set us free from the prejudices of education, and the burthensome yoke of Revelation. But for what purpose? unless to bring us into the wretched state of heathenism; that is, of doubt, of ignorance, of error, and perplexity. Whatsoever such disputers may affirm, none can be real friends to virtue, who are enemies to Christianity.

Let not therefore our constancy be shaken by those false pretences to clearer light, or

---

[m] 1 *Cor.* ii. 14.   [n] 1 *Cor.* i. 17.
[o] Such endeavours *to corrupt the simplicity that is in Christ*, (2 *Cor.* xi. 3.) the Apostle in one place calleth ἐν πειθανολογια, (*Col.* ii. 4.) in another, ἐν πειθοις ἀνθρωπινης σοφιας λογοις, (1 *Cor.* ii. 4.) that he might guard us against being seduced by such plausible specious reasonings, which are founded more upon the subtlety of evasions, and the arts or embellishments of style and language, than the force of truth and conviction.

greater knowledge. Of divine matters Reason alone is an incompetent judge, and can go no farther than opinion, which may be ill founded and erroneous: Now error in speculation is often the real cause, and more often the alleged and pretended cause of immoral and vicious practice. Let divine Revelation therefore, the unerring rule of our Faith have its perfect work; let it correct our opinions, and direct our conduct. Let us hold fast our profession, as we are taught; knowing from whom we have learned, and how sure and certain *the hope of our calling is* [p] *in Christ, who is both the power, and the wisdom of God* [q] unto Salvation.

[p] *Ephes.* i. 18.   [q] 1 *Cor.* i. 24.

SERMON IV.

Gal. III. 21. latter part.

—— *If there had been a law given, which could have given life, verily righteousness should have been by the law.*

THERE is no point, which the inspired writer of this Epistle hath more in view, than precisely to state the distinction between the law and the Gospel[a], and convincingly to display, by a

[a] Lex notat eam verbi divini partem quæ præceptis et interdictis constat, cum pollicitatione præmii erga eos qui dicto audientes sunt, et Comminatione pœnæ in immorigeros.

Evangelium significat doctrinam Gratiæ plenissimæque salutis in Christo Jesu, ab electis peccatoribus recipiendæ per Fidem. Witsii Animadversiones Irenicæ, cap. xvii. De prædicatione Legis et Evangelii, p. 218.

great variety of arguments, the manifest superiority of the latter. Being called to the apostolical office by the miraculous interposition of God himself, by an extraordinary *light from heaven, above the brightness of the sun* [b] in its meridian splendour: he was not *disobedient unto the heavenly Vision* [c]. Satisfied that the same high and Divine Authority which had, in so memorable a manner, *ordained him a Preacher, and an Apostle* [d], *was not of men, neither by man* [e], but was the direct immediate Revelation of God; he was the more unwearied in his labours, to inspire others with equivalent sentiments of the truth and importance of the doctrines he had received from so supreme and unerring an instructor.

When he addressed himself to the Gentiles, his aim was to demonstrate the absolute impossibility of their attaining the true knowledge of Religion from the weak efforts of Reason and Philosophy; which knowledge, in the present depraved and corrupted state of human nature, could

[b] *Acts* xxvi. 13. [c] *Acts* xxvi. 19.
[d] 1 *Tim.* ii. 7. [e] *Gal.* i. 1.

only

only be acquired by the communications of a divine Revelation. When concerned with the Jews, he pursued a different plan of argumentation: He acknowledged the divine Original of the Mosaical dispensation; but contended that they had overlooked and strangely mistaken the whole scope and intention of it, by a servile attachment to the external letter of it. They boasted, that in their law, distinguished ordinarily into moral, judicial, and ceremonial commandments, was contained every thing necessary to life and happiness: and that the punctual performance of the ritual ordinances gave them a sufficient plea of merit, to secure their acceptance with God. They were of the seed of Abraham; they had the promises of God; they were in the covenant with him, and therefore were undoubtedly entitled to the benefits of it.

In opposition to these assertions the Apostle maintained, that they only which *are of faith, are* to be reckoned *the children of Abraham*[f]*:* for the promise, being made to

[f] *Gal.* iii. 7.

him whilst *he was in* a state of *uncircumcision* [g], appertained equally to Gentiles and to Jews. True he granted it certainly was, that to render this promise more signally conspicuous, (however universally gracious the design of it was) it was not only appropriated to Abraham, but also particularly limited by God himself to a single individual of his family; *for he saith not, and to seeds as of many; but as of one, and to thy seed, which is Christ* [h]*:* thus making it to center in one person deriving his natural descent from him [i]. But it was through this extraordinary person, (he argued) that the great blessing exhibited in the covenant was to be communicated indifferently, and without respect of persons, to as many as should hereafter believe in his name. Such is the substance of the Apostle's reasoning contained in this and the subsequent chapter.

Indeed his whole design and intention, in this pastoral charge to the Galatian

---

[g] *Rom.* iv. 10.
[h] *Gal.* iii. 16.
[i] Doddridge's Family Expositor. Vol. v. p. 50. note (a).

church, is plainly calculated to confirm the peculiar excellency of the Gospel of Christ, to represent the blessings and privileges of it in the most engaging and affectionate light, and to vindicate it from the impositions of those Mosaical rites and ceremonies, which the new converts from Judaism were too apt to imagine, on account of their divine original, ought not to be suddenly superseded. This gave him the opportunity to enlarge upon the spiritual tendency of the Gospel; that *Moses was faithful as a servant*, in his delivery of the law of rites and shadows: *but Christ as a Son*[k], was in a superior light, the dispenser of grace and truth, the life and substance of the things testified beforehand concerning him by the Jewish Lawgiver. He exhorted them therefore *to stand fast in the liberty wherewith Christ had made them free, and not to be entangled again with the* burthensome ceremonial *yoke of bondage*[l]; a *yoke, which*, how long soever they had been habituated to it, *neither their fathers nor they were able to bear*[m].

[k] *Heb.* iii. 5, 6.   [l] *Gal.* v. 1.
[m] *Acts* xv. 10.

This was a favourite topick with him, and makes a principal part in thofe other Epiftles, wherewith he hath enriched the Church: He eagerly took occafion, when ever occafion offered, to magnify the grace of Chrift, and to explain the nature of *juftification by faith, without the deeds or works of the law* [n]. This alfo is the purport of the whole Epiftle to the Hebrews, which is generally imputed to him, as the writer of it, from the fimilarity of the arguments adduced to prove the impotency of the law, whether moral or Mofaical, to juftify men in the fight of God; for the *law made nothing perfect; but the bringing in of a better hope, by the which we draw nigh unto God* [o] and find acceptance with him, adminiftred and fupplied that which was wanting.

When this *better hope* was manifefted, as it was firft to be propofed to the Jews, it was incumbent upon the promulgators of it, to fhew its connection with their Reli-

[n] *Rom.* iii. 28.
[o] *Heb.* vii. 19.

gion.

gion. Many accordingly were convinced by referring to the things *witnessed by the law and the prophets* [p], and *believed the record which God gave of his Son Jesus Christ* [q]. But some of them, either unwilling or unable at once to relinquish all the prejudices of their education and their ancient principles, were earnest in their attempts to incorporate the rites of their old law with the works of their new faith; esteeming the former, which was confessedly of divine institution, of so sacred and uncontroulable authority, as never to be abrogated.

Against these erroneous notions, the having recourse again to servile *carnal ordinances* [r], *to weak and beggarly elements* [s], as they are expresly called, does our Apostle vindicate the law of Christ, and shews its pre-eminence over that of Moses; which was only meant as the introduction to it, and was to expire when that appeared. All who *waited for the consolation of Israel, all who looked for redemption in Jerusalem* [t], expected a purer and more spiritual Religion, to

[p] *Rom.* iii. 21.   [q] 1 *John* v. 10. 20.   [r] *Heb.* ix. 10.
[s] *Gal.* iv. 9.   [t] *Luke* ii. 25. 38.

abolish

abolish that variety of ritual services in their temple-worship; *which, to answer the wise ends of Providence, were imposed on the* Israelites *only for the destined time of reformation*ᵘ, and till that superior and ultimate dispensation appeared, which was so to correct and order all things, that they might best attain their perfect state.

For notwithstanding the foundation of the moral Law, and the Levitical religious observations were of God's appointment and direction; yet as they consisted chiefly of such lifeless external ceremonies, which did not reach the inward man, they could not confer peace and pardon of sins, or certainty of eternal life. *If such a law had been given, which could have given life* by man's perfect obedience to it, *verily righteousness should have been by the law.* But, says the Apostle, so far is the law from introducing any justifying righteousness, that *the Scripture hath concluded all*ʷ, both Jews and Gentiles alike, *under sin,*

ᵘ *Heb.* ix. 10.
ʷ *Gal.* iii. 22. Συνεκλεισεν i. e. declaravit omnes Homines conclusos et captivos teneri sub potestate et dominio Peccati, mortisque ac damnationis reos. Stockius sub voce κλειω.

shut

shut them up together, as so many condemned prisoners; *that the promise made to Abraham, that in his seed shall all the nations upon earth be blessed*[x]*, might be given to them that believe,* and trust in that method of justification and acceptance, *which should afterwards be revealed*[y]. Hence, if they were made sensible of the misery of their fallen state, they might be delivered as well from the bondage of the natural law, which tended only *to darken the understanding, and to blind the heart*[z]; as from the laborious services of the Jewish law, which was now only to be considered as having been their rigid *schoolmaster to bring them unto Christ*[a] *: For all* men *are the children of God by faith in him*[b].

The many deficiencies and imperfections of the natural and moral law were the subjects of the last discourse. The words now before us evidently mark the same or equal defects

[x] *Gen.* xxii. 18. [y] *Gal.* iii. 22, 23. [z] *Ephes.* iv. 18.
[a] *Gal.* iii. 24. [b] *Gal.* iii. 26.

First,

> First, In the Mosaical or ceremonial law.

Therefore, from the manifest impotency of both, to make satisfaction for past offences, and to secure a title to eternal life, will follow,

> Secondly, The necessity of a better law, to ascertain these blessings.

After what hath been already remarked, a few observations will suffice to note the comparative weakness and unprofitableness of the Mosaical law, and its insufficiency to answer the great ends of life and salvation. First, because the original promises of this institution, taken independently of posterior declarations, or prophetical illustrations, were merely of a temporal nature; such as either related solely to the circumstances of this present life; or such, as when viewed in contradistinction to the law of grace, life, and spirit, may warrant us to term the institution itself an occasional dispensation. The hopes and future prospect

pect of the Jews were therefore confined within a narrow compass. From rigidly and pertinaciously adhering to the prescriptive ceremonial part of their Religion, as being of itself the available means of justification and salvation, they were thereby diverted from attending to the spirituality of the promises hidden under the obscure veil of types and allegories: so that the law was to them, in effect, little better than a dead letter. A future state, however the patriarchs and good men amongst them might possibly believe it[b], was not openly or in direct terms, so promulged to them, as to be made the clear object of their faith, or the certain reward of their obedience. Even with the advantages which we Christians derive from the knowledge *of better promises*[c], however it may seem deducible from other parts of the Old Testament, this doctrine is at best so obscurely expressed in the law, or rather scarcely more than alluded to; that it cannot plainly and absolutely be collected from it: insomuch, that it hath given occasion

[b] *Heb.* xi.
[c] *Heb.* viii. 6.

of much doubt and controversy among learned men, whether it made any part of the divine Legation of the Jewish legislator; as temporal rewards and punishments are apparently the only sanctions of the Mosaical covenant.

Secondly, The law was little more than a covenant of works; or, as our Apostle elsewhere terms it, *the law of commandments, contained in ordinances*[d]*:* Was an outward directory or system of polity, the supposed alliance between God and his church; consisting, for the most part, of precepts and injunctions to duty, which required a perfect rectitude of life, without imparting strength and assistance for the work enjoined. *It was not* the obedience *of faith* which was required; for what it promised, it promised not upon condition of believing, but of doing: *the man that doeth them, shall live in them*[e]. This induced the Jews to seek for pardon of sins by their own merit, by what was their own righteousness, by their own works,

[d] *Ephes.* ii. 15.
[e] *Gal.* iii. 12.

and

SERMON IV.

and by their own sacrifices; by such external observances as had no real excellency to recommend them, but the command of the legislator. Nor could the outward law, whose administration they were so zealously attached to, ever insure inward and unsinning obedience. Alas! if man in the full strength of his paradisiacal innocency could not remain perfect, where could his security be, when his strength was gone from him, and such rigorous demands made for the punctual performance of his duty.

From the amazing multiplicity of the precepts, from the very many injunctions respecting the particulars of their religious ceremonies, and from the several tedious circumstances, attending their *gifts and sacrifices*, their *meats, and drinks, and washings*[f], which were all enforced with very severe penalties, it was with great difficulty the Jews themselves could distinctly learn all the duties of their law: It was moreover next to an impossibility, that they could be conscientiously satisfied, whether

[f] *Heb.* ix. 9, 10.

they had performed them all in due prescribed order and manner; or whether, notwithstanding their great desire to fulfil the law, they might not have contracted some ceremonial impurity, if not moral also; and by that means might have reason to apprehend, that they were *not cleansed according to the* perfect *purification of the sanctuary*[g].

Such is the impotency of the law, with all its ordinances and institutions of worship, to procure that expiation of sin, the necessity of which was shadowed by those solemn representations. It enjoined an intricate course of formal, expensive, and troublesome duties, and required compleat and full performance of them all, without any security of remission, without any prospect of relaxation, or abatement. It deemed him who offended in one point, altogether guilty or obnoxious to the curse, and denounced on the transgressor this extreme malediction; *cursed is every one that continueth not in all things which are written in the book of the law to do them*[h]. Obe-

---

[g] 2 *Chron.* xxx. 19.
[h] *Gal.* iii. 10. referring to *Deut.* xxvii. 26.

SERMON IV.

dience to such a severe law, such a covenant of works, could not be paid by any of the sons of Adam, who are all found sinners against it. Justification therefore could not be attained under it, for then it *could have given life:* And consequently Christ, who died *to redeem us from the curse of the law* [i], must be *dead in vain* [k]. As the law could not thus *give life,* so neither could *it make the worshippers perfect, as pertaining to the conscience* [l]. It is upon this account styled in the apostolical language the *ministration of sin* [m], *of condemnation* [n], *and of death* [o]. In opposition to the law of grace by Christ, which is called *the ministration of righteousness, of glory, and of life* [p].

But moreover the Mosaical œconomy, though it derived its being and establishment from Divine Authority, was only local and temporary; it was not calculated for universal practice or extent. It was limited to a few, to a particular people confined within the district of Palestine,

[i] *Gal.* iii. 13. [k] *Gal.* ii. 21. [l] *Heb.* ix. 9.
[m] *Rom.* viii. 2. [n] 2 *Cor.* iii. 9. [o] 2 *Cor.* iii. 7.
[p] 2 *Cor.* vi. 9.

or the land of Canaan, a small, obscure corner of the world: It was the religion of those, who were within a proper distance of Jerusalem, where was the temple of God; and where all who feared the name of the Lord God of Israel, and hearkned to his voice, were obliged to resort so many times every year, to offer their sacrifices, and to perform the duties of divine worship. This was such a command, as the rest of the world could not possibly have complied with, who lived beyond the boundaries or jurisdiction of this favoured land: It was not, it could not therefore be intended for general acceptation; but only to separate and distinguish that chosen people from other nations; and to serve particular purposes of God's pleasure and providence.

But as this law was not universally extensive, so neither was it calculated for perpetual duration. It was to subsist no longer than a given predetermined period: The enforcement and obligation of its whole system, agreeably to antecedent declarations, were to cease, *when the seed should come,*

SERMON IV.

come, *to whom the promise was made* [q] : whereas had it consisted altogether of essential duties, they would not only have been for ever binding; but all people every where, and at all times, must have been alike subject to it. Such an eternal law was reserved as the peculiar privilege, the singular happiness of the Christian covenant. Christ the Messiah was foreordained to be the termination and accomplishment of all the statutes and ordinances of the Jewish institutions. *He was to make* full and perfect *reconciliation for iniquity: He was to bring in everlasting righteousness* [r] : He was to establish an universal *covenant* with mankind, *ordered in all things and sure* [s], and all people, nations, and languages were to be called to accede to it: For his *gospel* was to be *preached to every creature which is under heaven* [t] ; *that all men may come unto the knowledge of the truth* [u] ; and that in every nation, he that feareth God, and worketh righteousness, may assuredly *be accepted with him* [w].

[q] *Gal.* iii. 19.   [r] *Dan.* ix. 4.   [s] 2 *Sam.* xxiii. 5.
[t] *Col.* i. 23.   [u] 1 *Tim.* ii. 4.   [w] *Acts* x. 35.

From this comparative sketch of the defects both of the law of nature and of Moses, we see how uncertain the duties of the one were, and how difficult those of the other; how liable men were to mistake in the former, and how subject to death in the latter; the expediency therefore of a better law,

Secondly, Must be obvious and unquestionable. By the transgression of the law of innocency, man became subject to sin, and to death the inevitable consequence of it. He had offended his Maker, and needed an intercessor to effect a reconciliation with him. Continuing still to sin his own poor stock of virtue could plead but little in his behalf, and would be but a wretched foundation on which to rest his hopes of recovery from his fallen state. The law of nature could give him no information how this could be brought about: The law of Moses was little better than a covenant of condemnation. Neither of these laws could make *the comers thereunto*

SERMON IV.

thereunto perfect[x]*:* it being a vain imagination to expect, *that their righteousness could be fulfilled in us*[y], when so great and so general was *the infirmity of our flesh*[z]. Not being able to overcome the corruptions of nature, they leave us without the prospect of relief or remedy, subject to the terrors of their curses. And why? because they *were not of faith*[a]. God had appointed such a different method of reconciliation, as would gloriously exhibit his love to men, and testify their filial obedience to him.

By the rigid demands of the law, pardon or even compassion were excluded; the soul that sinned *died without mercy*[b]. The substitution of sacrifices might have taught men to apprehend the necessity of a piacular satisfaction, adequate to the removal of the evil of sin, and to purify that conscience, which would otherwise condemn them. The true and only way

[x] *Heb.* x. 1.   [y] *Rom.* viii. 4.
[z] *Rom.* vi. 19.   [a] *Gal.* iii. 12.
[b] *Heb.* x. 28.

of reconciliation was at length exhibited: Chrift the Meffiah appeared as the great and promifed deliverer from the wrath of God, and from the guilt and punifhment of fin. He was an advocate of prevailing efficacy, who could fupport his laws by his own exalted nature and authority: For he revealed more clearly, he fealed more powerfully, and brought to their intended perfection all thofe glorious truths and promifes, which were before but faintly fignified in the outward letter, and fymbolical reprefentations of the law. The law of works indeed was good in its time and place; but the law of faith was better in its foundation and in its end: It illuftrated, explained, and ripened the other: And when both are viewed together, they form that divine, confiftent, and harmonious plan by which the myftery of God and redemption is haftening to its final accomplifhment.

This happy concurrence was that miraculous evidence of God's good will to man, which occafioned the acclamations of admiring angels. A grateful fenfe of the
bleffings

blessings of this salvation, a conviction of the guilt and misery of mankind, an assurance, *that by the deeds of the law shall no flesh be justified*^c, made the Apostle dwell with rapture and delight upon this pleasing subject: *Him*, saith he, that is Jesus Christ *hath God set forth*, hath publickly exhibited^d, *to be a propitiation through faith in his* meritorious sacrificed *blood, to declare* or demonstrate^e *his righteousness*, or justifying power *for the remission of sins*^f.

Such is the nature and perfection of this better covenant, which gives us also the most compleat knowledge of our duty. What reason or the light of nature could do, is best known by what it really did do; having no sure foundation to build upon, it could form no regular system of

^c *Rom*. iii. 20.
^d προέθετο proposuit, proprie denotat ponere ante, sistere et stature in conspectu aliorum, &c. Inde transfert Paulus ad Christum, quem in veteri testameuto per umbram legis exhibitum, in novo in propatulo Deus posuit propitiatorium, atque per Evangelii Prædicationem in conspectu omnium stitit et manifestavit. Stockius.
^e Ενδυξις speciatim notat demonstrationem, qua aliquid ita dilucide ac manifeste demonstratur, ut appareat omnibus negarique nequeat. Stockius.
^f *Rom*. iii. 25.

Religion

Religion or Morality sufficiently persuasive to virtue, wisdom, and holiness. Who will presume to say, it is a matter of mere indifference, whether men have a clear and certain, or an obscure and fallible rule to walk by: a rule which cannot fail, or a rule which hath hitherto failed all mankind, the greatest, the best, and the wisest of all ages; the manifold defects of which are still visible, wherever revealed Religion hath not been taught, or established. Revelation alone distinguishes itself by so compleat a system of duty, as, when received, is able to convince the judgement, and to influence the practice. Our blessed Lord himself *fulfilled all righteousness* [g], all the precepts of the natural and the moral law: *In him were hid*, and from him did proceed as the incarnate wisdom of God, *all the treasures of wisdom and knowledge* [h]; and he hath left us his example as the best interpretation of his will, and comment upon his doctrines.

In truth, where can such effectual laws and motives to goodness be found as in

[g] *Matt.* iii. 15. [h] *Col.* ii. 3.

the Gospel of Christ? Where else are the promises of the spirit of grace, that divine extraordinary assistance which so enables and strengthens us in the performance of our duty, as that, if we are not wanting to ourselves, we shall *be presented holy, and unblameable, and unreproveable in the sight of God* [l] ?

There is another peculiar excellency in this better covenant, which indeed may be regarded as its greatest blessing and privilege; which is, the means of reconciling ourselves to God upon failure, and even upon repeated failure of duty, if we truly repent. Before the publication of these good tidings, who could have presumed upon the pardon of his sins? who could thought of so dear a sacrifice, so valuable a satisfaction for them as the death of the only begotten Son of God? that he should come into the world, *to give his life a ransom for* our sins [k], a ransom for our original, for our actual, yea for all our sins; *for God made him to be sin*, that is, a

[l] *Col.* i. 22.
[k] *Matt.* xx. 28.

sacrifice

sacrifice for sin, *for us, who knew no sin; that we might be made the righteousness of God in him* [1].

It is fully sufficient for our comfort and encouragement to be assured, that this doctrine cometh by the express Revelation of God: Nothing but his supreme authority could have convinced us that he had formed such *counsels of* mercy and of *peace*[m]; and that Christ's impeccable obedience, and meritorious sufferings were necessary for our redemption. Confiding in the plenitude of this testimony, we may remain satisfied with the apostolical assertion in the text, *that if there had been a law given which could have given life, verily righteousness should have been by the law.* But as *both Jews and Gentiles are all under sin* [n]; it is only by *the law of the spirit of life in Christ Jesus* [o], that we can have any hope *to be justified from all things, from which we could not be justified by* any other *law* [p], even by that righteousness which is of God by faith

[1] 2 *Cor.* v. 21. [m] *Zech.* vi. 13. [n] *Rom.* iii. 9.
[o] *Rom.* viii. 2. [p] *Acts* xiii. 39.

in Chrift [q], gratuitoufly made over and promifed to them who believe in him for Pardon and Salvation.

Who this illuftrious Perfon and Character is fhall be the fubject of the next Difcourfe.

[q] *Phil.* iii. 9.

SERMON V.

LUKE II. 11.

Unto you is born this day in the city of David, a Saviour, which is Christ the Lord.

MANY previous notifications, great and solemn preparations manifestly indicate, that uncommon and extraordinary circumstances are to be expected as attendant upon an event, thus formally and frequently predicted. Notices of this kind forcibly bespeak the attention of those to whom they are addressed, and for whose use and benefit they are more immediately designed; and powerfully excite them

them to contemplate the greatness and importance of the object in whom such wonders are to terminate.

From those several passages of Scripture which have been occasionally mentioned in the preceding Discourses, we find what various intimations and *promises God made unto the Fathers*[a], of their future acceptance and salvation; and that a long succession of Prophets was miraculously raised up, from time to time, to illustrate the office and kingdom, the grace and glory, of that exalted Person who should hereafter appear in the conspicuous character of the Messiah, the Redeemer of the world. With this view, every minute circumstance, relative to so sublime an object of faith and hope, was particularly pointed out; that *when the fulness of the time was come*[b], the completion of the prophecies might be a miraculous confirmation of their Divine Original and authority. Whereas, if the predictions, and their proposed accomplishment did not coincide, all that had been spoken

[a] *Acts* xiii. 32.
[b] *Gal.* iv. 4.

before-

SERMON V.

beforehand was spoken in vain, and tended only to deceive and to lead into error.

When man lost his innocency in Paradise, the benignity of his Creator did not long suffer him to feel the weight of his displeasure; he soon gave him joyful hopes of mercy and forgiveness. These hopes, in later times, were increased to the full assurance of truth and certainty, that *God would bring in everlasting righteousness*[c], and *reconcile all things to himself*[d]. From the view we have already taken of the merciful designs of Providence, and the methods made use of to accomplish this scheme of our redemption, we learn the necessity and vast importance of the knowledge of God in Christ. Hence do we also discover the pre-eminence of his Gospel over the efforts of unenlightened reason, and the improved, but still defective law of Moses. Hence are we likewise convinced on the surest grounds, that *all the promises of God in Christ are yea, and in him amen*[e], incontestably, invariably sure and faithful. To

[c] *Dan.* ix. 24.
[e] 2 *Cor.* i. 20.
[d] *Col.* i. 20.

manifest the transcendent nature of him, who was the declared *mediator between God and men*[f], those blessed Spirits that are round about the throne of God in the highest heavens, were required to pay their attendance upon him their Lord, in the several periods of his ministry upon earth. His conception was announced by the message of an angel; the divinity of his person was proclaimed by another at his incarnation; a voice from heaven declaring also his divinity, was heard at his baptism, and at his transfiguration; the angels of Bliss were the comforters of his humanity in his hours of distress, after his temptation in the wilderness, and in his agony in the garden; they also first imparted the welcome news of his resurrection and Ascension.

In the history of the chapter from whence the words of the text are taken, we find these angels, the delegated harbingers of his nativity, exulting as being the blessed instruments of publishing such good tidings of great and universal joy, which

[f] 1 Tim. ii. 5.

would

would accrue from this glorious event to the whole human race; those blessings of Salvation which *he* would bring, who is emphatically styled *the first begotten* [g], *the first born of every creature* [h], *and heir of all things* [i]: A multitude of the heavenly host is suddenly introduced singing praises to God for the birth of that gracious Being, in whose human nature the Deity dwelt, and who now *appeared to put away* or abolish *sin by the sacrifice of himself* [k], and to bring *glory to God in the highest, and on earth peace, good will towards men* [l].

And to whom were these celestial agents sent? to the great men of the world? No, in no wise. A few poor shepherds, engaged in their ordinary callings, and at that very time *keeping watch over their flocks* [m], had the earliest intelligence that this great blessing had actually taken place. To the *meek* [n] and *to the poor was the Gospel to be preached* [o]. It was first preached to these low and humble keepers of sheep; it was

[g] *Heb.* i. 6. [h] *Col.* i. 15. [i] *Heb.* i. 2. [k] *Heb.* ix. 26. [l] *Luke* ii. 14. [m] *Luke* ii. 8. [n] *If.* lxi. 1. [o] *Matt.* xi. 5.

afterwards publifhed to, believed in, and received by the world through the preaching of a few weak, friendlefs, unlearned Fifhermen; to convince the world, that the Almighty bringeth about his deep defigns by means contrary to human wifdom and policy; ufing, for the moft part, the meaneft and moft unlikely inftruments to accomplifh his grandeft purpofes; *that the excellency of the power may* more eminently appear to *be of God*[p], and not of man.

It may feem perhaps a matter of mere fpeculation, if a prophecy be, as to its main end or defign, unequivocally fufilled, to enquire, whether all the intermediate occurrences, which occafionally have happened, are of importance fufficient to engage an equal fhare of our notice: But in cafes of general import, in matters of fact, and where Deity avowedly hath interfered, no circumftances can appear minute or trifling which concern the veracity of God's promifes, or the certainty of our Faith. Thus in the angelical declaration before us,

[p] 2 *Cor.* iv. 7.

SERMON V.

the time and place of Messiah's nativity are equally ascertained with the divinity of his person: And this seems to have been done with an eye to the accomplishment of the ancient Prophecies concerning him, and more perfectly to establish the truth and reality of his manifestation in the flesh. *Unto you is born this day, in the city of David, a Saviour, which is Christ the Lord.*

Let us consider therefore,

1. The time,
2. The place,
3. The person,

here so particularly described.

From the great variety of previous references to a precise and determinate period, surmises of which were not confined within the narrow limits of Palestine, but had, by tradition or information, attracted also the notice of other nations; an universal expectation was raised throughout the world, of the appearance of some high and wonderful Personage in it, at the very time

time in which Christ was born [q]: For he was to be as much *the desire of all nations* [r], as the peculiar hope of those, *who looked for redemption in Jerusalem* [s].

The Jews, guided by the sure word of Prophecy, were very confident in their expectations of his approaching advent, at the very time when he appeared amongst them. Mistaking indeed the spiritual meaning, the true intention of the promises, they pleased themselves with the vain notions of a temporal Prince, who should restore the splendour of their fallen kingdom. This too readily disposed them to listen to the many pretensions of those various impostors and false Christs, which started up amongst them in those days. They knew *that Shiloh or Christ was to come, when the sceptre was departed from Judah* [t]. The destined period for the accomplishment of this Prophecy was now at hand. Herod an alien, an

---

[q] This is noticed by Tacitus, Hist. Lib. v. S. 13. and by Suetonius in Vita Augusti, S. 94. and in Vita Vespasiani, S. 4.

[r] *Hagg.* ii. 7.   [s] *Luke* ii. 38.

[t] *Gen.* xlix. 10. This was the first Prophecy which limited the time of Christ's Advent. All the three Targums concur in applying it to the Messiah. Many of the Jewish writers,

Idumæan by defcent, though a Jew by Religion, was their king or governor; but was fo appointed by the authority of the Roman Power, to which they were then tributaries. And not long after, when their temple and city were deftroyed, neither fceptre nor lawgiver remained amongft them. Well therefore might our blefled Saviour reproach the Jews for their blindnefs and hypocrify, in being *able to difcern the face of the Sky, but not the figns of the times* [u]; for their objection to him as the Meffiah, had no regard to the time of his appearance, but was levelled againft his perfon alone, as too mean and inconfiderable for that exalted character. *We know this man, whence he is* [w], and from whom defcended: *Is not this Jefus the fon of Jofeph, whofe father and mother we know* [x]? *but when Chrift cometh, no man knoweth whence he is* [w]. He is to be born of a Virgin in an unaccountable and wonderful manner; he is alfo to be the Son of God,

writers, ancient and modern, in like manner interpret it of him; as *Shiloh* is one of the names given to the Meffiah in their Talmud. This is obferved by all our Commentators.

[u] *Matt.* xvi. 3.   [w] *John* vi. 42.
[x] *John* vii. 27.

by a way ineffable and inconceivable. They therefore rejected him, without enquiring into the authentic relation of his preternatural conception, and without attending to the power and energy of his miraculous operations.

Daniel's LXX Weeks, that is, weeks of years, had fixed the precise time of his coming. Haggai[y] and Malachi[z] had as explicitly prophesied, that it should be before the destruction of the second temple; which upon that account, as being honoured by the personal presence of the Messiah, who taught his glorious doctrines, and who wrought many glorious miracles in it, should far exceed in glory all the wonders of the former.

But moreover this particular time, when Christ was to be born, not only answered the general Prophecies concerning that event; but if we attend to other considerations, it seems also the fittest opportunity for carrying on God's good pleasure in this

[y] *Hagg.* ii. 7. 9.
[z] *Mal.* iii. 1.

gracious

SERMON V.   121

gracious dispensation. When the greatest part of the known world was under one common empire, spoke almost all one language, were ruled by one law, united by the blessings of peace, and civilized by arts and learning, then were men at leisure to listen to and to search after truth; and likely to become more and more sensible of the weakness and wickedness of their own nature, so as to feel their want of a ray from heaven, and thence be induced to desire it, to illuminate their minds. Then was ushered into the world the blessed Prince of Peace, and Lord of Life and Glory, the *Emmanuel* [a] or *God with us* [b]; who became incarnate to perfect all the mysterious abysses of God's decrees, and to procure par-

---

[a] עמנו אל. A name expressive of the union of the two natures in Christ: of his converse, as man, with men upon earth; and of his spiritual presence, as God, with his people *always, even unto the end of the world.* Matt. xxviii. 20. Novimus enim ex hoc nomine, 1. quod salvator noster sit verus homo. Est enim nobiscum, nobisque ομοουσι⊙. 2. quod sit verus Deus. Est enim אל Deus fortis. 3. quod sit una persona, Deus et Homo. Est enim Deus nobiscum. Et si consideretur hoc nomen ratione officii salvatoris, Paulus inquit, 2 *Cor.* v. 19. Deus erat in Christo, mundum reconcilians sibi . . . . . sic in Christo et per Christum Deus iterum nobiscum est: Hic est Scala Jacobi, in qua Angeli ad nos descendunt, et Deus ipse desuper gratiæ ocellis nos respicit. Glassii Opuscula Christologia, p. 414.   [b] *Matt.* i. 23.

don,

don, reconciliation, and redemption for us. At this time, the very state of things in the world could not but contribute greatly to give those blessings a readier entrance, and to facilitate the more extensive propagation of the Gospel [c].

2. But as the time, so likewise is the place, in exact conformity to scriptural predictions, particularly mentioned, where this Saviour of mankind was born. The Prophet *Micah*, six hundred years before the time, had pronounced *Bethlehem Ephrata* by name, the scene of this event, to distinguish it from another *Bethlehem* in the tribe of *Zabulon* [d]; whereas this *Bethlehem* is specified in the book of *Ruth* to belong to the tribe *of Judah* [e]; and accordingly St. *Matthew* and St. *Luke* in their histories call it *Bethlehem of Judæa* [f]. Here *came forth*, or was born, *that ruler in Israel, whose goings forth*, whose generation and

---

[c] Jortin's Discourses concerning the Truth of the Christian Religion, 2d Ed. p. 175.
[d] *Josh.* xix. 15. [e] *Ruth* i. 1, 2. [f] *Matt.* ii. 1. *Luke* ii. 4.

SERMON V.

fonſhip, *have been of old from everlaſting* [g]. Of this we have moſt undeniable vouchers. *By the determinate counſel and foreknowledge of God* [h], the Roman emperor had ordered a ſurvey to be taken, and a taxation to be made in all the provinces of the empire. This brought the Virgin and Joſeph *to Bethlehem the city of David* [i]; that, being of that houſe and family, they might alſo be regiſtred as citizens of that place. *While they were there, the days were accompliſhed that ſhe ſhould be delivered* [k]; and there was Jeſus born.

By this it is manifeſt how human circumſtances or ſubordinate cauſes, without any previous knowledge or foreſight, act in ſubſerviency to God's predeſtinating will

---

[g] *Mic.* v. 2. ומוצאתיו מקדם מימי עולם, are words ſufficiently eſtabliſhing as well the human nativity, as the eternal generation of Chriſt. קדם frequently ſignifies proper eternity. Thus *Deut.* xxxiii. 27. God is called אלהי קדם. In *Pſalm* lv. 20. he is ſaid וישב קדם. In *Habak.* i. 12. the Prophet aſks, הלוא אתה מקדם. So that whilſt *the coming forth of this Ruler out of Bethlehem* points out particularly the reality of his humanity; his *goings forth being of old from everlaſting*, do as diſtinctly denote his eternal generation and ſonſhip by the promiſe of God, before ever the heavens and the earth were made.

[h] *Acts* ii. 23.   [i] *Luke* ii. 4.   [k] *Luke* ii. 6.

and

and commands, and execute his decrees. Such use doth he make of men as his agents, without their having any suspicions of it. Thus whilst the emperor of Rome pleased himself in carrying on his own schemes of worldly power and policy, he was effectually confirming the truth of ancient Prophecies, and demonstrating the subjection of the Jews to his dominion: And his own Registers, those public Records of the State, became so many convincing evidences of the notoriety of the fact, that Jesus was born in the place which was marked out by the Prophets, and is called in the text *the city of David*[1].

---

[1] Many are the appeals which the apologists and other ancient writers, in the earlier days of Christianity made to these publick Registers. Justin Martyr, who lived about the middle of the second century, in his dialogue with Trypho, mentions this taxation of Augustus; but in his first apology, he particularly refers to the censual tables to prove that Christ was born at Bethlehem, and was of the family of David. Ὡς και μαθειν δυνασθε εκ τ̅ απογραφων τ̅ γ[ε]νομενων επι Κυρινιȣ τȣ υμετερȣ εν Ιȣδαια πρωτȣ γενομένȣ επιτροπȣ. Apol. 1. ad Antonin. Pium. S. 44.

Tertullian, at the expiration of the same century, in several of his works, refers to the same Records as the most indisputable authority: More particularly, in his fourth book against Marcion he repeatedly appeals to them, as to the best vouchers for the truth of this matter. In his seventh chapter he says, De censu Augusti, quem testem fidelissimum dominicæ nativitatis Romana archiva custodiunt. In his nineteenth chapter

From the time and place of Christ's nativity proceed we to consider,

. 3.: The dignity and excellency of his person, as pronounced by the Angel to be *a Saviour, Christ the Lord.*

He shall be the Mediator of a new and better covenant between God and man, He shall save his people from their sins, is the constant voice of Scripture and Prophecy from the Fall to the Redemption. By deriving our being from the loins of a transgressing progenitor, we are born under the controuling influence of his fallen and

---

chapter he refers to them for further information—apud quos (census scilicet actos sub Augusto) genus ejus inquirere potuissent. In his thirty-sixth chapter he thus expresses himself. Tam distincta fuit a primordio Judæa gens, per tribus et populos et familias et domos, ut nemo facile ignorari de genere potuisset, vel de recentibus Augustianis censibus adhuc tunc fortasse pendentibus.... Qui vult videre Jesum, David filium credat per Virginis censum. Long after these, Chrysostom, who flourished at the close of the fourth century, in one of his Sermons or Homilies upon Christmas-Day, appeals to those very Registers as still extant in his time, in the following words. Καὶ τοῖς ἀρχαίοις τοῖς δημοσ.κ κειμ[ένοις] Κωδιξιν επι της Ρωμης εξεστι εντυχοντα, και τ καιρον τ αποχραφης μαθοντα ακριβως ειδεναι τ βυλομβρον. κ. τ. λ. Homil. in Christi Natal. Tom. 5. p. 512, 513. Ed Sav.

corrupted

corrupted nature, subject to the sentence and condemnation awaiting sin unpardoned, and totally unable of ourselves to make any equivalent satisfaction. What we could not do for ourselves, Christ did for us. He became man, that as man he might *fulfil all Righteousness* ᵐ. " Taking to him-
" self our flesh, and by his incarnation
" making it his own flesh, he had now of
" his own, although from us, what to
" offer unto God for us. And as Christ
" took manhood, that by it he might be
" capable of death whereunto he hum-
" bled himself; so because manhood is the
" proper subject of compassion and feeling
" pity, which maketh the sceptre of his
" regency even in the kingdom of heaven
" amiable, he which, without our nature
" could not on earth suffer for the sins of
" the world, doth now also by means
" thereof both make intercession to God
" for sinners ⁿ, and exercise dominion over
" all men with a true, a natural, and a
" sensible touch of mercy °." So greatly *hath God commended his love towards us, in that*

ᵐ *Matt.* iii. 15.   ⁿ *Heb* iv. 15.
° Hooker's Ecclesiastical Polity, B. v. S. 51.

while

while we were yet sinners, Christ died for us [p], and paid the price of our Redemption; that thus being delivered from the common dangers of personal and original evil, we might become members of that mystical body whereof he is head, and thereby be entitled to that eternal glory and happiness which he hath purchased for us. *For him hath God exalted to be a Prince and a Saviour, for to give repentance and forgiveness of sins* [q], *and power to become the Sons of God, even to them that shall believe in his name* [r]. Indeed, the very name Jesus [s] indicates

---

[p] *Rom.* v. 8.   [q] *Acts* v. 31.   [r] *John* i. 12.

[s] *Jesus*, or God the Saviour. *In nomine Jesu* (says the pious John Arndt) *totum Evangelium comprehenditur.* A name the same as, and derived from the Hebrew יהושע: A word compounded of יה the common contraction of יהוה, which denotes a being necessarily existing, and which hath being in and from himself; and חושע, which signifies a saviour or Deliverer, without defining or determining his nature; יה therefore directly points out the absolute inherent divinity of JESUS, who, as the true יהושע could perfect and compleat that character typified in the Old Testament by that הושע, whose name was changed by divine designation into this distinguished appellation יהושע. v. Num. xiii. 16. *Nulla scripturæ differentia distinguens hoc Christi proprium nomen ab ejus nomine qui Mosi succedens populumque ducens in terras promissas Christum, æternæ quietis datorem, non tantum nominis sono sed et rebus gestis adumbravit. ut videre est,* Act. vii. 45. *et* Heb. iv. 8. v. Grotii Annot. in Matt. i. 21.

a Sa-

a Saviour[t], the divinity of whose power *can save us with an everlasting Salvation*[u].

2. But this *Jesus* the *Saviour* is here called *Christ,* or, which is the same word, *Messiah,* to denote his appointment or consecration by unction, to that high office which he had undertaken to execute. This was the usual initiatory ceremony which distinguished the prophetical, the sacerdotal, and the regal character[w]. Thus the Prophets, when entrusted with any commission of singular importance, were anointed with *oil poured upon them*[x]. Thus, was the high priest consecrated to his sacred function *by holy anointing oil*[y]. Thus also were their kings inaugurated into their exalted office[z]. Other nations have, in like manner, adopted this religious ceremony, and from hence have kings themselves been dignified with the honourable

---

[t] *Matt.* i. 21.   [u] *Is.* xlv. 17.
[w] Sometimes indeed persons are spoken of as delegated to these offices, without the ceremony of any external anointing, yet are said to be anointed to such offices. See Archbishop Secker's Lectures on the Catechism. Lecture VII.
[x] 1 *Kings* xix. 16.   [y] *Exod.* xxix. 7.
[z] 1 *Kings* xix. 15, 16. 2 *Kings* ix. 6.

appella-

SERMON V.

appellation of the Lord's anointed. Thus was the Saviour of mankind set apart and consecrated to his several offices of Prophet, Priest, and King. He was that *Prophet like unto Moses, to whom all men were required to hearken*[a]. *He was a Priest for ever after the order of Melchisedek*[b]. He was *that King whom God* of old *promised to set upon his holy hill of Sion*[c]. As *the tabernacle, the ark, the altars*, and all things pertaining to them were sanctified by the effusion *of oil, and made most holy*, and as *whatsoever touched them was holy*[d]: So did the spirit of *Jehovah*, when *Jesus* assumed humanity and became invested with his mediatorial office, fill him with gifts and graces of the *Spirit without measure*[e] or limitation: so that *from the anointing which we receive of him*[f], *from* the overflowing *fulness* of his essential divinity, *do we* his people *receive grace for*, or upon *grace*[g]; deriving from him that illumination and *unction which teacheth us all things*[h], which sanctifieth us wholly, and by that means

[a] *Deut.* xviii. 18, 19.   [b] *Heb.* v. 6.   [c] *Psal.* ii. 6.
[d] *Exod.* xxx. 26—29.   [e] *John* iii. 34.   [f] 1 *John* ii. 27.   [g] *John* i. 16.

maketh

maketh or confecrateth *us to be Kings and Priefts unto God and his Father* [i].

3. To thefe two appellations of a *Saviour*, and of *Chrift*, is added a third of fimilar, if not fuperior magnitude, the title of *Lord*, to denote his power and fovereignty over all things. This is the peculiar ftyle of our mafter in the Scriptures, *the Lord* or *our Lord*. Thofe rapturous words of the Pfalmift, which are fpoken by way of apoftrophe to the Son, *thy throne O God is for ever and ever* [k], are produced by the argumentative writer of the Epiftle to the Hebrews [l], as wholly applicatory to him, and to contain a clear and full defcription of him, his ftate, and his mediatorial kingdom. *Thou haft crowned him with glory and honour, and haft put all things in fubjection under his feet*, is the prophetick teftimony of the fame devout writer to Meffiah's future grandeur, and is applied by the fame infpired interpreter [m], to the perfon of Chrift, as denoting the extent, ftability, and perpetuity of his dominion.

[i] *Rev.* i. 6.   [k] *Pfal.* xlv. 6.   [l] *Heb.* i. 8.
[m] *Heb.* ii. 7. citing *Pfal.* viii. 5, 6.

Such

Such and so great is the supremacy of his power and authority, that it cannot be subverted, or himself removed from his throne by any, or by all his enemies; unlimited power in heaven and earth being given unto him. Moreover we are his subjects, his servants, and his creatures by every right and claim: And he is declared our Lord, our Master, and our God by every style and title, whether of inheritance, or purchase, or election, or conquest.

All this is signified under the denomination applied by the Angel to the holy child Jesus, when he was proclaimed to men as their great and adorable *Lord*. An appellation invariably bestowed upon Christ by all the sacred penmen of Scripture, whenever there is occasion to name either his person or his office: as if the spirit of Prophecy foreseeing the violent opposition which would arise in later times against the eternal existence, the inherent divinity of the Son of God, was peculiarly anxious to remove every objection, that human wisdom, or rather human weakness might presumptuously urge against it: for surely pure and absolute Deity cannot be spoken of in terms of any other signification, or in words of sublimer and more mysterious import, than what are ascribed to *Jesus* when declared to be, by the attestation of such competent witnesses, *a Saviour, Christ the Lord.*

This also is the testimony he gave of himself and of his own original powers, when he severally affirmed, that he *came forth from God*[n]; that he *was his Son*[o]; that *what things soever the father doth, these also doth the Son likewise*[p], from the unity of their essence, and their omnipotence: So that *they who had seen him, had seen the Father also*[q]; as he was *the express image*, the visible representation or resemblance *of his Person*[r], and to whom was joined the spiritual, invisible, divine Nature of the most high God; for he was truly and literally God incarnate, God and man. In his converse with men, he divested himself of his greatness, *and took upon him the form of a*

[n] *John* xvi. 28.   [o] *John* iii. 16.   [p] *John* v. 19.
[q] *John* xiv. 9.   [r] *Heb.* i. 3.

servant;

servant [t] : But notwithstanding this external humiliation and abasement, he could not relinquish his real nature, his peculiar dignity; for he was, and could be no other than the Son of God, though *made in the likeness of men, and found in fashion as a man* [t]; and therefore *he thought*, or counted *it no robbery*, or usurpation of a prerogative which did not properly belong to him, *to be equal with God* [u], or to assume those incommunicable names, titles, and attributes, by which the Almighty hath made himself known; and to require from men the homage and adoration due to that supreme Being.

To these distinguished glories of their Master, his Apostles with grateful joy bear their concurrent evidence. They assure us, that after Christ had offered up himself to God, as the meritorious and propitiatory sacrifice for sin, *he entered into heaven itself, now to appear in the presence of God for us* [w], as our all-sufficient and prevailing Advocate and Intercessor. There they re-

---

[t] *Phil.* ii. 7, 8. [u] *Phil.* ii. 6.
[w] *Heb.* ix. 24.

present him placed at the throne of God, not like a petitioner standing in a posture of humble reverence before it, but as partaker of coessential and coeternal glory with the Father, sitting down upon it *on the right hand of the* glorious *majesty* of God [x], or, as the same inspired writer afterwards expresses it, *on the right hand of the throne of the Majesty in the heavens* [y]. In this place, which is the more peculiar residence and manifestation of the presence of God, is Christ described as invested with an amazing plenitude of power; and all the celestial inhabitants which are round about the throne of God are spoken of as falling down and worshipping him that sitteth upon it; and *calling upon every creature which is in heaven, and on the earth*, and upon universal nature, to add their joyful acclamations in concert with the whole choir of Angels and of Saints *to him that sitteth upon the throne, and to the Lamb for ever and ever* [z]; even to that mystical *Son of man, who is the first and the last; he that liveth and was dead: and is alive for evermore* [a]: he who was declared

[x] *Heb.* i. 3.   [y] *Heb.* viii. 1.   [z] *Rev.* v. 13.
[a] *Rev.* i. 17, 18.

to be the Son of God with power [b]; and tho' slain and *crucified* by *enemies (who would not that he should reign over them* [c] *)* yet *hath God made him both Lord and Christ* [d].

From these considerations, from the intrinsick greatness of Messiah's person, gifts, and graces, we are called upon by every tye of reason and of duty, of gratitude and of affection, to rejoice and bless God for the miraculous incarnation of his Son. If holy men of old, if patriarchs and prophets *saw this day* at a distance *and were glad* [e]; if they who had only an obscure vision, a faint representation *of the glory which was to follow* [f], could *rejoice with joy unspeakable* [g], how much exceeding theirs must our transports be for the full manifestation and accomplishment of those promised mercies. Blessed are *our eyes for they see, and our ears for they hear the things which Kings, and Prophets*, and wise Men *desired to see and hear* [h], without the happiness of having their wishes compleated; *God having provided better things*

[b] *Rom.* i. 4.   [e] *Luke* xix. 27.   [d] *Acts* ii. 36.
[c] *John* viii. 56.   [f] 1 *Pet.* i. 11.   [g] 1 *Pet.* i. 8.
[h] *Luke* x. 24.

for us, under the Gospel covenant; and hence having determined, *that they without us should not be made perfect* [1]; but that he would finally *bring* all his *sons unto glory* [k], even unto the full consummation of their hopes through *Christ,* their *Saviour* and their *Lord.*

By this Revelation of divine Philanthropy did God make known all the mysterious secrets of his Providence, all the momentous articles of grace and truth, of light and life, and so make them known, *that all the ends of the earth have seen,* and may become partakers of *the salvation of God* [l]. If therefore deliverance from all evil, spiritual and temporal; if the announcing of peace, pardon, and reconciliation between God and man be tidings of joy and comfort; if the promises of good and happiness infinite and eternal be desireable and delightful, then should his name who secured all these inestimable blessings be for ever dear and precious to us. With the utmost rapture and thankfulness should we

[1] *Heb.* xi. 40. [k] *Heb.* ii. 10.
[l] *Psal.* xcviii. 3.

praise

praise and magnify him as the source and fountain of all good here, and of all hope hereafter. For in him *mercy and truth have met together* ᵐ; heaven and earth, God and man were united to bless and to save us.

This is the true foundation of devotion, praise, and love. This will teach us with equal extasy to repeat the Hosannahs of the Angels, and to sing *glory to God in the highest, and on earth peace, good will towards men* ⁿ. With the heavenly Host we shall chant our grateful Hallelujahs, *for the Lord God omnipotent reigneth* °. We shall with exulting hearts give our tribute of joy, honour, and adoration, because *the kingdoms of this world are become the kingdoms of our Lord, and of his Christ, and he shall reign for ever and ever* ᵖ : *having redeemed unto God by his blood* the sons of men *out of every kindred, and tongue, and people, and nation* ᑫ. These are the wonders which *Jesus* hath done for us, who was a *Saviour*, even *Christ the Lord*.

ᵐ *Psal.* lxxxv. 10.   ⁿ *Luke* ii. 10.   ° *Rev.* xix. 6.
ᵖ *Rev.* xi. 15.   ᑫ *Rev.* v. 9.

SERMON VI.

JOHN v. 23. latter part.

——*He that honoureth not the Son, honoureth not the Father which hath sent him.*

IT is obvious to remark that the Gospel of St. John is distinguished by a peculiar simplicity of style, by a concise and definite form of expression, and by a familiar diction of the utmost plainness in its grammatical construction: Nevertheless it must be acknowledged, that many of the doctrines and propositions therein delivered are difficult to be comprehended by the human

human mind, and more difficult to be interpreted and explained by mere human abilities. The reason of this difficulty is also plain and obvious; since however simple and easy may be the general style, yet the words are often metaphorical and figurative: And we need not wonder, that the Evangelist should adopt this method, and so far condescend to human infirmity, when he is delivering the sublimest truths, and declaring the ineffable mystery and œconomy of the divine wisdom in the wonderful work of man's redemption. The other Evangelists, for the most part, contented themselves with delivering the historical narration of what Christ did and suffered, or those things which chiefly ascertained the reality of his human nature: But St. John who probably survived all the other Disciples of the Blessed Jesus, and lived long enough to see heresies and false doctrines creeping into the Church, and threatening the peace of it, formed his Gospel upon a different plan. In the very introduction of it, he asserts in the most absolute and unlimited terms the divinity and eternal pre-existence of the *Word* or *Logos*,

Logos, which word was our *Jesus*; and that all the several interesting characters of *light, life, truth, grace,* and *glory,* did most eminently center in, and marked the person of the *word made flesh*[a]: His incarnation also is related in words of singular import and enforcement, more fully to inform us of the gracious purposes for which the Deity was pleased to assume in a visible bodily shape our human nature.

After this solemn and emphatical declaration of the original glory and dignity of the *word*; to evidence his own convictions, and to keep up the impressions they would naturally excite, the Apostle, in the course of his history, takes peculiar pleasure in the recital of those remarkable occurrences of Christ's life and ministry, which more immediately tended to magnify his inherent grace and power, which openly manifested him to be, in a very significant and appropriate sense of the words, *the Son of God, God* himself incarnate, *dwelling* or pitching his tabernacle *amongst us,* and exhibiting the last

[a] *John* i. 14.

and most glorious appearance of his Shechinah upon earth. Not that there are wanting in the other sacred historians sufficient and ample proofs to establish this leading and fundamental article of our faith. They did not however so professedly enter into the discussion of it; but as occasion might sometimes incidentally lead them, they confirm it, by using such expressions, which, compared with other Scriptures, cannot consistently be otherwise interpreted: for they seem to take it for granted that it never could be called in question; and was naturally deducible from the consideration of those miracles which Jesus did, and from the view of those Prophecies they pointed out, as indisputably fulfilled in him.

But alas! no sooner did Christianity gain ground, than terms of art and doctrines of human philosophy began to be mixed with it; and errors concerning the person, nature, and offices of Christ, were industriously spread and eagerly embraced. To obviate these alarming mischiefs, our Evangelist, who was honoured with the most

intimate

intimate confidence of Christ whilst upon earth, was present at every memorable transaction, and was a frequent witness of his divine glory, was best qualified to give the most satisfactory account of his antecedent glory and greatness, and to expose the error and malignity of those perverters of the Faith, who asserted that he was but a mere man. This, which he was best able to do, he hath done in his Gospel: In the very beginning whereof he discovers his opposition to the rising Heresies of that age, by advancing such positions as irrefragable maxims, which are in the fullest repugnancy to the principles maintained by the abettors of them; and which it is his direct purpose throughout the whole to demonstrate to be false.

In the progress of his history, in the farther narration of those amazing operations which sufficiently vindicated the divine authority of the blessed Jesus, and evidenced *his glory* to be *the glory as of the only begotten of the Father*[b], he produces a great

---
[b] *John* i. 14.

variety of proofs to illustrate his grand object, that *Jesus was the Son of God*. In the chapter from whence the words of the text are taken, we are informed that our blessed Lord having miraculously healed *an impotent man on the sabbath day*, justified the propriety of this action from the objection of its being a profanation of that holy day, by asserting his unity and equality in nature and operation with his Father: *My Father*, says he, *worketh hitherto, and I work* [c]; not as an inferior subordinate instrument, but as a principal efficient, jointly working together with him. He assumed no improper claim in thus calling God, πατερα ιδιον, not in a figurative, but an appropriate sense, his own peculiar Father. As his Son he was *Lord also of the Sabbath* [d], and to be looked upon in that superior light. That the Jews, who were present at this miracle, might by it be convinced of his divinity, he represented to them in the most unequivocal terms his absolute equality with the Father, from the following considerations, because both are equal

[c] *John* v. 17.
[d] *Mark* ii. 28.

SERMON VI.

in operation, will, and consent; for *what things soever the Father doeth, these also doth the Son likewise*[e]. From the affection which the Father beareth to him; for he *loveth him, and sheweth him all things that himself doth*[f]. From his omnipotency, in raising the dead by the same essential authority and freedom of will; *for as the Father raiseth up the dead, and quickeneth them: even so the Son quickeneth whom he will*[g]. From his power of judging the world, which *the Father hath committed unto the Son*[h]; and from his partaking of the same original principle of life with the Father; *for as the Father hath life in himself, so hath he given to the Son to have life in himself*[i], in the same independent and equal degree. To these arguments in proof of his unity of essence, and equality in power, glory, and dignity with the Father, he addeth, as competent witnesses to corroborate them, the several testimonies of *John the Baptist*[k], of his own works[l], of *the Father which had sent him*[m], and *of the Scriptures*[n].

---

[e] John v. 19.   [f] John v. 20.   [g] John v. 21.
[h] John v. 22.   [i] John v. 26.   [k] John v. 33.
[l] John v. 36.   [m] John v. 37.   [n] John v. 39.

Upon thefe authoritative credentials of his divine origin and miffion, with the greateft propriety and juftice might our bleffed Lord fay, it was incumbent upon all men, *that they fhould honour the Son, even as they honour the Father;* for, certainly *he who honoureth not the Son,* invefted with fuch exalted powers, *honoureth not the Father which hath fent him.*

In the farther confideration of thefe words we will enquire,

>Firft, Who may be reckoned to honour not the Son.

>Secondly, Why fuch, in reality, honour not the Father.

The more exalted and the more glorious the worth and dignity of the Redeemer's perfon and character are, the more, furely, hath *God commended his love towards us* [o]. Not thankfully to accept his gracious over-

[o] *Rom.* v. 8.

tures thus recommended, muſt argue a low eſteem of Chriſt, and all the precious promiſes of God in him. We need not however go beyond the pale of the Chriſtian Church to find out thoſe who honour not the Son of God. They who live in open violation of his moral laws, do practically diſhonour him, are a reproach to his Goſpel, and to that ſacred name of his whereby they are called. Others may alſo effectually diſhonour the Son of God, who ſhall neglect or ſlight any of his poſitive inſtitutions, deeming the obſervation of them a needleſs act of duty, and that it is a matter of mere indifference whether they are adminiſtred or not. Surely they who thus think and act with regard to ſuch ſolemn indiſpenſable ordinances, and preſume to treat them either with ludicrous mirth, or to explode them with pretended argument, may not unjuſtly be reputed to entertain in reality the ſame low opinion of him, who appointed theſe as the diſtinguiſhing ceremonies of his Religion, as they profeſs to have for the obligation of the rites themſelves.

We may delude ourselves with vain imaginations; we may amuse ourselves in forming many plausible and ingenious schemes of Salvation; yet none will approve itself so certain in its principles, so rational in its institutions, so easy in its practice, so forcible in its motives, and so conducive to virtue and happiness, as the full scheme of Redemption exhibited in Scripture. Yet how frequently have weak and rash mortals taken upon them to correct and improve this gracious dispensation, by cutting off what they fancy to be superfluous, or by adding what they judge still wanting to its compleat perfection; artfully endeavouring to obtrude into the world, not so much the pure, plain, and unadulterated Religion of Christ, as that modification of it which they have adventured to suit to their various refinements. Thus whilst some have so mystically spiritualized the Gospel, as almost, if not entirely, to divest it of external institutions, and to leave no apparent signs, no distinguishing marks of a Church or religious Service: Others, in the contrary extreme, have

have so loaded it with numberless ceremonies and superstitious fopperies, as to make it consist of little more than a constant round of outward shew and form, a tiresome repetition of useless and unedifying rites. Both parties at the same time styling themselves Disciples and followers of the blessed Jesus; both equally dishonouring him and his holy Religion; both making the inventions of men, not the word of God, the controulers or discriminative characteristicks of the laws and precepts of Christ.

But moreover, and principally, Christ may be dishonoured if his divinity be denied. This sort of dishonour is what we may presume the Apostle chiefly aimed at in the text; and is in effect to reduce him to the level of created beings, and to divest him of that eternal *glory, which he had with the Father before the world was*[p]. For he either is, or is not God. If he be God, to call in question his divine inherent excellencies, and to refuse him the honour

[p] *John* xvii. 5.

due unto him, will, in its consequences at least, fall little short of Atheism itself. If he be not entitled to that divine character, it will be an equal offence against God to ascribe those perfections to Christ, which do not in reality belong to him. But can we allow ourselves to suppose that the Saviour of mankind, who came into the world as well to promote the honour of God, as the happiness of men, would upon any account, and without any reservation, have *made himself equal with God* ^q, and pronounced *that he and his Father are one* ^r; if he was absolutely nothing more than a finite creature existing in time, and had no such equality with the Father, and no communication or participation of the Deity with him? Or would he, in justification of such mysterious language, have ventured to reprove the Jews for their religious indignation against him, because he plainly claimed supreme essential Divinity as his just prerogative, by this remarkable vindication of his assertions; Shall *ye* presume to *say of him whom the Father hath sanctified*, or so-

^q *John* v. 18.
^r *John* x. 30. and xvii. 11, 22.

lemnly

lemnly confecrated *and sent into the world in such an exalted light, thou blasphemest, because I said, I am the Son of God*[s]? Behold, *I do the* miraculous *works of my Father*[t], which clearly demonstrate a divine agency; *that ye may know and believe that the Father is in me, and I in him*[u], by such an intimate indissoluble union, as will fully warrant the strongest deductions you can draw in proof of my divinity from such high, uncommon, and mysterious expressions.

The ancient Scriptures represent the Almighty as jealous of his honour: *my glory,* says the Lord by the Prophet Isaiah, *will I not give to another*[w]; to another, or to a strange God, or to any being who hath not the name and nature of the Deity. To these Scriptures did Christ appeal in his behalf: The constant mode or tenor of his speeches was such as no subordinate being would dare to use. The Jews well knew that *Son of God* and *Messiah* were convertible terms, signifying one and the same person.

[s] *John* x. 36.   [t] *John* x. 37.   [u] *John* x. 38.
[w] *Is.* xlii. 8. xlviii. 11.

This honour he claimed: and he who could affirm that *all things were delivered unto him of his Father: and no man knoweth the Son but the Father: neither knoweth any man the Father, save the Son*[x]; had a right to require that they who *believe in God, should believe also in him*[y]. If they doubted of his words, they could not however doubt or deny his works, those infallible proofs of his divinity; for *they* who heard and saw them *were amazed at the mighty power of God*[z]; well knowing that *no man could do those miracles which he did, except God was with him*[a]. With such signal tokens of divine favour and approbation, if Christ was not what he so solemnly declared he was, we must suppose, what we must almost tremble to mention, that God suffered his name and authority to be usurped by, and to vouch for an impostor. In the plainest construction of the words, this would be to rob God of that supreme honour which is due solely unto him, and to lead men into the grossest errors in the very essentials of Religion, nay, into idolatry itself; and

[x] Matt. xi. 27.   [y] John xiv. 1.   [z] Luke ix. 43.
[a] John iii. 2.

that

that even by him, *who*, when arraigned *before Pontius Pilate* the Roman governor for assuming the highest honours and titles, *witnessed this good confession* [b], that he *came into the world, that he should bear witness unto the truth* [c].

But *God manifested in the flesh* [d] hath ever been *a stone of stumbling, and a rock of offence* [e] to the wise men of the world. Not that, though owned to be an inexplicable mystery, they can prove it to imply any contradiction in terms, or any absurdity in the supposition. Such abstruse speculations, from the very weakness and imperfection of our faculties, must necessarily be involved in some degree of obscurity, and be viewed, as distant objects are, by reflection, *through a glass, darkly* [f]. We know no more how matter and spirit act upon each other, than we know the mystery of the Deity: but that they do, is certain; that the soul actuates the body, we feel and ex-

[b] 1 *Tim.* vi. 13. [c] *John* xviii. 37. [d] 1 *Tim.* iii. 16.
[e] 1 *Pet.* ii. 8.
[f] 1 *Cor.* xiii. 12. Εν αινιγματι per ænigma, i. e. orationem obscuram, cujus verba quidem audiuntur, sensus autem non percipitur. Stockius.

perience; and that, from the impulse of outward objects, it receives numberless ideas: but in what manner, is a mystery in nature, and as much above the reach of our understanding, as any thing which the Scriptures assert of the being and nature of God. That there is such an all-wise, and almighty, and all-perfect being, is unquestionable; but it is beyond the bounded capacities of the human mind, to form an adequate idea of the nature of his essence, or the mode of his existence.

When therefore we find the highest names and titles, and all the known incommunicable properties and attributes of the Deity ascribed to Christ by the inspired Writers of the Scriptures; may we not reasonably infer, that Jesus, whose Disciples we are and whose Religion we profess, is that very God whose works we admire, and whose majesty we adore? In those divine oracles of grace, and wisdom, and truth, there are so many passages, which either positively affirm, plainly inculcate, or tacitly imply, that Christ is the very and eternal

SERMON VI. 155

eternal God; *the first and the last*[g]; from everlasting to everlasting: *He which is, and which was, and which is to come*[h]; *the almighty*; *the same, yesterday, to day, and for ever*[i]; that it must require great chicanery, and great sophistry, to controvert and explain away such forcible evidences. Indeed from the variety of subterfuges, and withal from the frequent concessions of some of the greatest opposers of this Doctrine, who scruple not occasionally to acknowledge, that there never was a time when the Son did not necessarily exist; we may form some judgement of their embarrassment, and of the violence they must have done to their religious principles, before they could prevail upon themselves totally to reject the ancient uniform interpretation of every Church professing Christianity, from the apostolical age to the present days[k].

[g] *Rev.* i. 17. [h] *Rev.* i. 4. 8. and iv. 8.
[i] *Heb.* xiii. 8.
[k] Mr. Whiston himself could once say, though he afterwards became a professed Unitarian; " I believe and am obliged so
" to do, that our Saviour Christ is truly Θεάνθρωπος, God and
" man; because I find it every where plain and evident, that
" the style, titles, attributes, actions, and incommunicable
" names of the eternal Deity, the God of Israel, are at least as
" frequently ascribed to him the Son, as to the Father himself,
                                                " throughout

Such disputers may perhaps deem themselves powerful pleaders in behalf of what they term Reason and Common Sense, whilst they tauntingly pronounce that " Ig-
" norance and Superstition may think to
" screen themselves behind the veil of
" mystery . . . . but a small degree of ra-
" tional reflection will convince us, that
" Revelation and Mystery are in their very
" natures as diametrically opposite to each
" other as Christ and Antichrist, Light
" and Darkness[1]." Such is the boasted Christianity of one who professes himself a sincere Disciple of Jesus Christ. *Nay but, O man, who art thou that repliest against God*[m]*?* Shall the person saved say, why hast thou saved me thus? Shall we not be content to be saved, unless we perfectly ap-

---

" throughout the whole Bible; notwithstanding any inability
" of comprehending the nature of God, and thence of judging
" of the unity or plurality of Persons in the Divine Essence."
                      Whiston's Theory of the Earth, p. 42.

[1] The Doctrines of a Trinity and the Incarnation of God examined upon the Principles of Reason and Common Sense. By a Member of the Church of England from birth and education, and a sincere Disciple of Jesus Christ from choice and rational conviction. Octavo, 1772, Chap. i. Section i. p. 78, 79.

[m] *Rom.* ix, 20.

prehend the whole progress of the Divine Dispensations respecting our Redemption; and, unless the nature and wisdom of God be accommodated to our own fond reasonings, and the shallowness of our own understandings? Why then are doctrines of Faith made necessary conditions of Salvation? Or shall we doubt and reject the truth and wisdom of God's Dispensations, because his love is greater than our conceptions; although we are expresly told it is so in his word [a]? The unbelieving Jews, who were as unwilling as any modern objectors, to allow the truth of what they could not comprehend, or to acknowledge the divinity of the person, and the excellency of the powers of Christ, whom they saw *made in the likeness of men* [o], were assured by him; with a solemn asseveration, (which enhanced their guilt in rejecting him,) that *before Abraham was, I am* [p]. The meaning of these words they could not misunderstand. " It is the very same expression, which " is used to express the eternity, and neces- " sary existence of the supreme God [q]."

[a] *Rom.* xi. 33. [o] *Phil.* ii. 7. [p] *John* viii. 58.
[q] Dr. Randolph's Vindicat. of the Trinity, Part II. p. 7.

If the devout followers of Christ, in obedience to his commands, are desirous *to honour the Son, even as they honour the Father;* and who, that they may retain the utmost reverence and awe for the person of their Redeemer, shall piously confess that he was as truly the Son of God before all time, as the Son of Man in time; will it convince them of the " folly, the unreasonableness, " the absurdity, or the nonsense of such be-" lief," to be harshly told, that the " esta-" blishing the Doctrine of the Incarnation of " of God, effectually established Idolatry in " the Christian Church'; and that the Doc-" trine of the inseparable Union of the two " natures in Christ, the blending together in " one compound or monstrous being, the di-" vine and the human nature; is not only " an absurd fiction, but an impious, and " even blasphemous doctrine˙?" But is this the way to promote the glory of God, or the credit and advancement of Christianity, by undervaluing and speaking lightly of the honour of its blessed Founder? if the Laws

---

ʳ The Doctrines of a Trinity, &c. p. 140. note.
ˢ P. 105, 106, and 169.

SERMON VI. 159

and Institutions of Christ have too little influence over those who chearfully look up to him, as the prevailing *advocate with the Father*[t]; as *his beloved Son, in whom he is well pleased*[u]; *and whom he will always hear*[w]: Certainly they will have much less weight with those who are taught, and are accustomed to consider him in the diminishing light of an inferior, subordinate, dependent creature; and at best only a mere human teacher of righteousness[x].

---

[t] 1 *John* ii. 1.   [u] *Matt.* iii. 17.   [w] *John* xi. 42.

[x] The warm and eager advocate for the Unitarian System above alluded to, is so vehement a contender for the supreme prerogatives of human reason and understanding, that he scruples not to aver, "that if they be not the rule of our reli-"gious Faith, it must be human folly and superstition:" (Chap. i. Sect. i. p. 78.) ostentatiously magnifying the "im-"portant services which would be done to the great interests "of virtue and uncorrupt Christianity, by him who, with an "honest freedom, would expose the obvious folly and bane-"ful superstition of some of the present *orthodox* and legally "established Doctrines of our Church." (Prefatory Address, p. 10, 11.) To promote this good design, this writer throughout his book, in very exceptionable language, repeatedly accuses "our Religion of Idolatry and falshood, begot by the su-"perstitious converts from the Greek academy, upon a few "figurative expressions of the sacred writings." (Pref. p. 43. Nay further, in another place he says, "I am bold to "repeat, that, notwithstanding the verbal and manual "assent of so many thousands of all ranks and ages, which "hath been supposed to be given to it; it is impossible for "any man really and *ex animo* to have believed the whole "of the first article of the Religion of our Church, for no man "ever did, or can believe it." (Ch. i. Sect. i. p. 57. The

same

SERMON VI.

What could animate the primitive Saints and Martyrs so patiently to suffer and so bravely to die, as the confidence that their Saviour was their God? It was this which afforded consolation to the first blessed Mar-

---

same improper language is again repeated in p. 80.) "To tell us therefore that the Father and the Son are but one and the same being, or that the Son is coeval with the Father, is to subvert at once every idea those words are used to convey to our minds; so that when we hear of a Son *of one substance and eternity* with his Father, the sounds indeed are familiar; but it is as impossible for us to comprehend the sense, should there happen to be any, as if it were a language totally unknown to us." (P. 66, 67.) But his presumption proceedeth to greater lengths, when he indecently pronounceth, "that every professor of our holy Faith, who worshippeth Jesus Christ as the very and eternal God, is actually a gross Idolater.... By the absurd superstitious Doctrine of a Trinity, and the pretended Incarnation of the Deity, by which two different natures, by a kind of theological chymistry, became amalgamated into one Christ, our most pure and amiable Religion hath received a foul and dreadful wound, under which she hath languished above fourteen centuries, sickly, feeble, and for the most part impotent." (P. 73. note, and p. 141. note. Pretended Incarnation, Prefatory Address, p. 41.) He having before observed, that "the so celebrated hypostatic Union, and the conceit of God's descending from heaven, and taking our nature upon him.... is derived from the source of heathenish idolatry." (P. 105.)

But accusing and reviling will not pass for arguing. Softer words would have been more becoming in a serious writer upon solemn and important subjects, and not in the least have hurt his cause. Where able and good men are engaged in a controversy, an humble and diffident one would carefully refrain from any expressions which may give disgust or offence: well knowing how many of equal worth and

tyr St. Stephen, under the bitter agonies of a moſt cruel death. He *ſaw the heavens*

and virtue, and full of the fame honeſt deſires to promote the ſacred cauſe of Truth and Religion, think differently from him in theſe articles. Indeed according to ſuch principles, here is an end at once put to the neceſſity of Revelation; if reaſon, or rather private judgement, be thus made the all-ſufficient teſt of a divine Faith. If this be ſo, the leſs per-feƈt evidence of Goſpel Light muſt give way to the clearer information of man's unerring all-comprehenſive underſtanding. But is this the truth as it is in Jeſus? *Ephef.* iv. 21. Or rather, is it not another Goſpel? *Gal.* i. 8. For we have not ſo learned Chriſt. *Eph.* iv. 20. Can teachers of ſuch a ſpirit make us wiſer and better Chriſtians? Do they reſtrain wiſdom to themſelves? *Job* xv. 8. And are they alone beſt qualified to teach and explain the laws of their Redeemer, as being perfeƈtly acquainted with the ſublime and heavenly Doƈtrines of his Revelation? Or are they ſuch eminent proficients in ſpiritual knowledge, as to be ſufficiently able to convince the world, that Articles of Faith are little better than ſo many unneceſſary impoſitions, ſo many tyrannical incroachments upon Chriſtian liberty, and ſo dreadfully offenſive to tender conſciences?

But enough has been ſaid already to confute the poſitions of theſe champions for human reaſon, though not enough to convince them of their errors. Whilſt we are in this ſtate of pilgrimage, we muſt expeƈt to walk by faith, and not altogether by ſight. What is neceſſary for us to know is adapted to our capacities of knowledge: What is above our capacities, or, thoſe ſublimer Doƈtrines of the nature, grace, and deſigns of God, we muſt acquieſce in the ignorance of, and admit them, ſo far as revealed, upon the ſole credit of God's word. No demonſtration, as Mr. Chillingworth hath well obſerved, can be ſtronger than this, " God hath ſaid ſo, therefore it is " true," (Rel. Pro. Ch. vi. Seƈt. lvi.) So that the only queſtion in this caſe need be, whether the Scriptures teach the doƈtrine or not? If they do, it muſt be received, however the wit of man may labour to throw upon it the veil of inconſiſtency, or cloath it with foreign and unnatural abſurdities.

L

opened,

opened, and the glory of God, and Jesus standing at the right hand of God [y] ; whose sacred name he ardently invoked, and unto whose saving power he recommended his departing spirit. So triumphantly did Faith in *Jesus*, as *the Son of God*, disarm the rage and terror of persecution, how ingenious soever in the invention, or barbarous in the execution of a vast variety of torments: And in a short space of time this well-grounded *Faith*, this *word of God so mightily grew and prevailed* [z] over all opposition, *the Lord confirming the word with signs following* [a], that princes themselves became its steady guardians and powerful protectors.

But no sooner was the glorified and exalted nature of the Son of Man called in question, and men became eager to be *wise in their own conceits* [b]; than discord and shedding of blood, and every evil work brought indelible infamy upon the Christian Church, though miraculously planted, and peaceably established. Hence controversies arose, which first corrupted the Faith, then vitiated the morals, and finally

[y] *Acts* vii. 55, 56.   [z] *Acts* xix. 20.   [a] *Mark* xvi. 20.   [b] *R o.* xii. 16.

destroyed

destroyed the most flourishing Churches in the world.

It was this spirit and love of Dissension which, in the earlier ages of the Gospel, so readily paved the way for Mahometanism in the East; and those churches which were once the glory of their times, soon fell a prey to the rapid progress of an impious impostor. The intemperate discussion of this sublime doctrine made a sad breach in the unity of the Faith; and those who became indifferent whether they adhered to it or not, easily got over their scruples, and hesitated not publickly *to deny the Lord who bought them* [c].

No sooner also was the Protestant Reformation of the Church effected in later ages, but the like disgraceful feuds commenced afresh, and being new modelled into Socinianism, occasioned equal disturbances. The churches of Hungary, Poland, and Transylvania, where it chiefly prevailed [d], (as had

---

[c] 2 *Pet.* ii. 1.
[d] Lampe Historia Ecclesiæ Reformatæ in Hungaria et Transylvania; and Dr. William Berriman's Moyer's Lectures, Sermon VIII. throughout.

happened

happened before to those of the East) experienced similar devastation and ruin, from those magnifiers of human reason and deniers of the virtue and merits of Christ's satisfaction, the proud scorners of this world, who will not be persuaded to *cast down imaginations* or vain reasonings, *and every high thing* or ambitious display of that false wisdom, *which exalteth itself against the knowledge of God*; not aware of the necessity of this humility of the mind, and how earnestly they are admonished to *bring into captivity every thought*, every presumptuous arrogant notion, *to the obedience of Christ*[e]. In good truth, this prurient spirit of controversy, this attempt to reduce *the deep things of God, which no man knoweth, but the spirit of God*[f], to the standard of human judgement and apprehension, hath been infinitely more baneful to truth and religion, than all the malice and persecutions of the most inveterate enemies to the cross of Christ.

[e] 2 *Cor.* x. 5. Λογισμὲς καθαιρὲντες Ratiocinationes evertentes, eas nimirum, quæ sunt contra Deum et mysteria divina. Steckius.
[f] 1 *Cor.* ii. 10, 11.

Those

Those indeed, who thus despise or deny the Divinity of the Son, profess however that they are actuated by no other motive than their zeal for the honour of the one supreme God and Father of all; which honour, if ascribed to the Son, is absolutely paying him that divine worship, which belongs wholly and solely to the Father.

This brings us to consider,

Secondly, The other clause of the words before us, that *they who honour not the Son, honour not the Father which hath sent him.* The connexion and union between them is such, that the honour is mutual and reciprocal; and that reasoning which establishes the homage due to one, confirms it also as due to the other. Very little therefore need be added to illustrate this point. By whatsoever prophet or preacher of righteousness God speaketh to man, he must be received in that light in which God shall reveal him: to disparage the office or person of such a messenger, must be a slight shewn to him who sent him.

If the spirit and voice of Inspiration represent *Christ as the only begotten and the beloved Son of God; the character, the likeness, the image, the form, the nature, and the manifestation of him* from all eternity, so as none other ever was, or, without the imputation of blasphemy, could be said to be; then it must be no inconsiderable offence against God himself, so to debase the honour of his Son, as to consider him as a finite dependent Being, of a nature different from and inferior to the Father. As a Son he is *one with his Father*[g], having the same common undivided nature, essence, properties, and attributes with him: and what greater honour can redound to him, than when the meritorious efficacy of our Redemption is considered to proceed from his own inherent and original grace, will, and power?

[g] *John* x. 30. xvii. 11, 22.

Nay,

Nay, it must be the greatest impiety to suppose, that God would suffer such a stumbling block to be laid in our way, as certainly is laid in Scripture, if Christ, with all these peculiar tokens of true and proper Divinity, be nothing more than a mere man, a created, precarious being, which he must be, if he be not truly God. Can we possibly and seriously imagine, that those sacred penmen, who wrote as they were moved by the Holy Ghost, would deliver most essential, necessary, saving truths, in so vague and careless a manner, as almost naturally, from the tendency of their reasonings, and tenor of their expressions, to lead us into the grossest errors of Polytheism and Idolatry, which would be the fact, if Christ is not to be looked up to as God?

Let us not however have less reverence for Jesus, than *Pilate* himself shewed, who, *when he heard that he had made himself the Son of God, was the more afraid*[h]. Let us

[h] *John* xix. 7, 8.

not join with the Jews in their clamours against him, *because that he being* in appearance *a man, made himself God*[i]. Contemplating only with the eye of weak and fallible reason the external view of his humanity, let us not insultingly say unto him, with his fellow-sufferer the impenitent malefactor, *save thyself and us*[k]. Alas! can this man of sorrows in his abject abasement presume *to think it not robbery* now, *to be equal with God*[l]; behold *he hath no form, nor comeliness, nor beauty,* nor strength, nor power, *that we should desire him*[m]? However worldly sceptical wisdom may judge thus, let us remember, that it was necessary for the Saviour of the world that he might *bring many sons unto glory, to be made perfect through sufferings*[n]. And that " the world's Salvation was, without the " Incarnation of the Son of God, a thing " impossible; not simply impossible, but " impossible, it being presupposed that the " will of God was no otherwise to have " it saved than by the death of his own " Son [o]."

[i] *John* x. 33.   [k] *Luke* xxiii. 39.   [l] *Phil.* ii. 6.
[m] *If.* liii. 2.   [n] *Heb.* ii. 10.
[o] Hooker's Eccles. Pol. B. v. S. 51.

SERMON VI.

Well therefore might Christ himself say, *blessed is he whosoever shall not be offended in me* [p]. And what saith the Spirit of the Gospel, of Faith, and of Love? This will teach us, that to acknowledge and confess *Jesus to be both Lord and Christ* [q], to be God and Man, will inspire us with the liveliest sense of joy, gratitude, and hope. Then shall we *honour the Son, even as we honour the Father: Angels, and Authorities, and Powers being made subject unto him* [r]. After many repeated messages by Prophets and holy Men of old; last of all *God sent his own Son* into the world, *in the likeness of sinful flesh* [s], saying, *they will reverence my Son* [t], the sovereign Lord and heir of all things.

With such extraordinary declarations from heaven to evince this article of our Faith, how chearfully may we trust to the merits of Christ's person, to the efficacy of his Intercession, and to the

[p] *Matt.* xi. 6. and *Luke* vii. 23.
[q] *Acts* ii. 36. [r] 1 *Pet.* iii. 22. [s] *Rom.* viii. 3.
[t] *Matt.* xxi. 37.

power

power of his Grace and Salvation; when we consider him as that great, glorious, and adorable Being, *who proceeded forth, and came from God*[u]; *who was with God, who was God*[w], and in whom *dwelt all the fulness of the Godhead bodily*[x]: Who, by his

---

[u] *John* viii. 42.   [w] *John* i. 1.

[x] *Col.* ii. 9. "Every word in this paſſage carries along "with it a peculiar force. For it is not ſaid, that the fulneſs "of the *Divinity* lodgeth in Chriſt, but of the *Deity*, or God- "head, the word not being θειοτης, but θεοτης. Nor is it "ſimply ſaid θεοτης, but της θεοτης, to aſſure us, that we "are to underſtand the Deity here in the higheſt ſenſe. Nor "yet is it barely ſaid, that he has πληρωμα, *a fulneſs* of the "Deity, but το πληρωμα *the fulneſs* thereof. But, as if it "were not enough to ſay *the fulneſs*, by way of eminence, "it is called παν το πληρωμα, *all the fulneſs*. Beſides, it is "not ſaid, that this all-fulneſs of the Deity *lodgeth* in Chriſt, "but the very contrary; that, κατοικει εν αυτω, *it dwelleth in* "*him*, as in its proper houſe, ſeat, or repoſitory. And all "this is ſtill more conſiderable, becauſe it is added, that the "all-fulneſs of the Deity or Godhead dwells in Chriſt σωμα- "τικως, *bodily*, or as ſome render it, ſubſtantially or really. "However the meaning is, that this all-fulneſs of the Deity "dwells in Chriſt, not as in the tabernacle and temple "of old, *emblematically* and *efficiently* only: Not under the "notion of *a general or univerſal Preſence or Providence*; "for ſo it is every where: Nor under the idea of a *ſpecial* "*efficiency of the Spirit*; for ſo God dwelleth in his Saints. "But we are to underſtand it of a real and proper inhabita- "tion, and ſuch as denotes a true perſonal union; ſuch an one "is peculiar and appropriate to the *Logos*, in conjunction "with the man Jeſus, with whom he has united himſelf." Fleming's Chriſtology, V. 3. p. 625, 626.

moſt intimate union with the Deity, is the object of our Obedience, our Worſhip, and our Faith, and *is over all, God bleſſed for ever. Amen*[y].

[y] *Rom.* ix. 5.

SERMON VII.

Rom. x. 10.

With the heart man believeth unto Righteousness, and with the mouth confession is made unto Salvation.

THE great Apostle of the Gentiles, in this elaborate part of his Epistle to the Roman converts, is earnestly solicitous to establish the profession of Christianity upon the firmest foundation, as well with regard to the inward persuasion of the mind, as the outward conformity of the practice. His address was to
Jews

Jews rigidly tenacious of the customs of their fathers; who imagined themselves secure in the principles of their Religion, because they were of the seed of Abraham, and therefore born within the covenant which God made with him and his family; and also, because the law itself was more peculiarly confirmed to them, in the observance of which they expected to be justified.

To convince them of their mistakes in these particulars, the Apostle assures them, *that they are not all Israel, which are of Israel*[a]: for *the children of the flesh are not the children of God: but the children of the promise are counted for the seed*[b]. Nay, moreover, that this very law, on which they thus relied for justification, was insufficient for that purpose; *because they sought it not by Faith, but as it were by the works of the Law*[c]. In reality, it had higher views and a further end, namely, to direct their fiducial regards to Christ; whose Gospel, superseding the works of

---

[a] *Rom.* ix. 6.   [b] *Rom.* ix. 8.
[c] *Rom.* ix. 32.

the ceremonial Law, was to be preached to all men, as well to Gentiles as to Jews, as a compleat everlasting covenant necessary for Salvation and final Acceptance with God.

This sounded harsh to those who, knowing the divine original of their Law, could form no idea of any other Righteousness, but what arose from obedience to that Law. Whoever discharged his duty in that respect, did, in their opinion, as much as God or man could require of him. In answer to this the Apostle argued; that they quite mistook the intention of their own Law, if they looked not, through it, to Christ: That Abraham himself, their illustrious ancestor, sought justification upon the very terms of that Gospel which he was recommending to them, viz. by Faith in the promises of God: That, as these promises were made to him *when he was in uncircumcision*[d], both *Jews* and *Gentiles* were included in them; for *he is the God of them both*[e], and all *have peace with him*[f],

[d] *Rom.* iv. 10. [e] *Rom.* iii. 29.
[f] *Rom.* v. 1.

being

being justified by the same means; by a Righteousness derived solely from Faith in *our Lord Jesus Christ, who is the end of the Law for Righteousness to every one that believeth*[g]. This new and better Covenant, not of works, but of grace, was now manifestly revealed; and true faith in Christ, with sincere confession of him, were henceforth made the stipulated conditions of Salvation.

The Jewish zealot might startle at the apprehension of its abolishing his old Religion, and all the ritual Ordinances of the Sanctuary. The Gentile philosopher also, from seeing no images, no altars, no sacrifices, might be equally offended at a Religion so void of pomp and shew: And though he set no value upon it himself, he could not bear to see his ancient superstition run down; if for no other reason, but because it was established by Law[h]. Both

[g] *Rom.* x. 4.
[h] Ego eas, (opiniones scilicet, quas a majoribus accepimus de Diis immortalibus, sacra, cæremonias, religionesque) defendam semper, semperque defendi: nec me ex ea opinione, quam a majoribus accepi de cultu Deorum immortalium, ullius unquam oratio aut docti, aut indocti movebit. Cicero de Natura Deorum, L. iii. S. 2.

however

however were called to relinquish their prejudices, and to accede to that real Religion which required them to *worship God in spirit and in truth*[1].

Not that from hence they, or any other future adversaries, should conclude, that Christianity consisted wholly in mental, spiritual graces; or that, if a man had what he thought the answer of a good conscience from within, was inwardly persuaded of the rectitude of his actions, there was no occasion to shew any outward conformity to the requisitions of his Faith; or indeed, to make any publick acknowledgement or confession of the Religion which he had embraced upon the principles of reason and conviction.

To guard against the mischiefs of so dangerous a delusion, the Apostle expressly assures his new converts, that as Faith is the root of all inward Religion, so confession is the necessary outward demonstration of it: *for with the heart man believeth unto*

[1] *John* iv. 24.

Righteousness, and with the mouth confession is made unto Salvation. In the preceding verse, the order of the words is inverted; where, speaking of the only way to obtain Righteousness or Justification, he advances this position: *If thou shalt confess with thy mouth the Lord Jesus, and shalt believe in thine heart, that God hath raised him from the dead, thou shalt be saved*[k]. But though the words may be transposed, the doctrine and signification of both are the same: Clearly importing, in the language of a late valuable expositor, that " God hath given
" a very plain and intelligible Revelation
" in his Gospel; and the substance of it is
" this, that *if thou* dost *confess with thy*
" *mouth, that Jesus is the Lord, and at* the
" same time *believe in thy heart,* with a
" vital and influential Faith, *that God hath*
" *raised him from the dead,* in proof of his
" divine mission; *thou shalt* assuredly *be*
" *saved.* .... For it is *with the heart* that
" a man *believeth to Righteousness,* or so as to
" obtain justification; nor can any thing
" but a cordial assent secure that; *and with*

[k] *Rom.* x. 9.

" *the*

SERMON VII.

"*the mouth confession is made to Salvation,*
"and that publick profession of Christia-
"nity is maintained, without which a secret
"conviction of its truth would only con-
"demn him [1]."

This is the Doctrine enforced in the words before us, which shall be further considered, by reflecting,

> First, Upon the nature and necessity of that inward principle of Faith requisite for our Righteousness or Justification.

> Secondly, Upon the equal necessity of a publick confession of it.

Whatsoever is revealed in the Gospel, is most undoubtedly the object of a Christian Faith, and demands our assent upon the evidence of that divine Authority. But though it be universally acknowledged, that it is as much the duty of Christians to believe, as to obey; yet many

---

[1] Doddridge's Family Expositor, Vol. IV. in Loc.

amongst us have widely differed in their notions concerning the nature of this belief. Some have looked upon it in no higher light, than as the bare assent of the mind to the credibility of divine Revelation: Thus making it no more a virtue to believe what is related of Christ in the Scriptures, than what is recorded of eminent persons in the annals of common historians.

Others, on the contrary, contemplating the excellent commendations ascribed to Faith, the exalted privileges, and the glorious rewards hereafter promised to it in Scripture, have no less hastily concluded it to be the sum and substance of Religion itself: And that nothing more is necessary to compleat our final Salvation, but an implicit acquiescence in whatsoever they persuade themselves comes recommended to them by so distinguished an appellation. Both these extremes are absurd and dangerous. True evangelical Faith is neither that which ariseth from a view of historical evidence only; nor is it so meritorious as to secure to us happiness and life eternal,
without

without the concurrent testimony of those "good works, which spring out necessari- "ly of it, insomuch, that by them a lively "Faith may be as evidently known, as a "tree discerned by the fruit[m]:" It is not a bare speculative notion of God and Religion, or yielding our assent to matters of fact undeniably proved. It is not only the settled conviction of our reason, but it is the inward persuasion of the heart and affections; by which it thus becomes the true principle of all virtuous active obedience.

Considered in this light, the Christian Faith, so necessarily instrumental to justification, is not so much a natural as a religious principle. It is a grace which disposeth us to a ready and immoveable trust in God; to a belief in his word, and to an unfeigned submission to his authority. It is paying an awful deference to the word of God, as such; and not as the result of any human testimony, which is weak and fallible; and our credit thereunto would

[m] Art. XII.

be more concerned with the matter than with the divine evidence. And though knowledge and understanding are requisite to the perfection of it; yet as its peculiar character is an assured confidence and a joyful hope, arising as much from the affections, as from the understanding; it teaches us silently to adore that wisdom, love, and mercy of God, which we cannot adequately comprehend, or fully express.

True it is, that from misunderstanding the doctrine of Justification, many unhappy doubts and disputes have arisen amongst Christians concerning the nature, mode, and degrees of it: Some contending warmly for the sufficiency of good works; others as zealously maintaining the all-powerful efficacy of Faith; each pleading apostolical authority, to exclude what is equally with the other the necessary condition of justifying Righteousness. There are also those, who not attending to the difference between divine and human Faith, but supposing them both to spring from the same fountain, and to be supported by the same evidence, have been too much inclined to look upon a fiducial assent,

as

as a kind of affront upon the human understanding, and an intolerable encroachment upon the liberty of private judgement: It being the first axiom in their school, that Reason alone is the measure and standard of Truth, and a perfect and compleat rule of duty in all cases, both towards God and man. Most assuredly an implicit bigotted adherence to the doctrines or opinions of men is shamefully base and servile; and altogether to regulate our judgement, and to form our conduct upon the conceits and authority of others, of any sect or party, is inconsistent with the dignity of Reason, and the liberty of Christians. But, nevertheless, this very principle which, when considered with respect to men, is pitiful and mean; in regard to God, is virtuous and honourable.

If we are satisfied with the authority which enjoins the several articles of our belief, it must be a most presumptuous offence to dispute their truth or to refuse our assent, because we do not perfectly see and understand the reasonableness or necessity of those injunctions, or are not able to conclude decisively concerning them. Abraham,

ham, who is distinguished as the Father of the Faithful, paid an absolute unreserved submission to the will of God, when he left his own *country and kindred*[n], *and went out not knowing whither he went*[o]. Nay, when his Faith was put to its strongest trial, and he was commanded to sacrifice his Son, the beloved child of his old age, and the special heir of promise, he did not argue, but obeyed; *being strong in faith, giving glory to God*[p], he doubted not; but *against hope believed in hope*[q].

If there be any virtue, merit, or praise in Faith, it must consist in putting our full trust and assurance in the promises of God, in a chearful resignation to his authority as such, without the vain attempt to explore or to account for all the dispensations of his providence, or the whole reason of his laws. " For as nothing finite has reality
" enough to represent infinite, so neither can
" any thing finite have capacity enough to
" comprehend it . . . A finite Being there-
" fore must have a finite understanding, and
" a finite understanding must have a finite

---

[n] *Acts* vii. 3. [o] *Heb.* xi. 8.
[p] *Rom.* iv. 20. [q] *Rom.* iv. 18.

" per-

SERMON VII.

"perfection [q];" or there could be no difference between beings perfect and imperfect, finite and infinite. In all cases, the veracity of *God that cannot lye* [r], nor deceive, is our sufficient security. To rest our assent upon this, is fixing it upon the very *pillar and ground of the truth* [s], whose foundation standeth firm and sure, for *its builder and maker is God* [t]: So that we may confidently say with the Apostle, *I know whom I have believed* [u], even him, who is able to make us perfect, *thoroughly furnished unto all good works* [w].

Such is the true Christian Faith so essentially necessary to Salvation, and so certainly productive of good works. Animated with this vital principle, we shall not remain indolently satisfied with a secret mental persuasion only; but as we have believed with the heart, so shall we,

Secondly, See the necessity of evidencing these convictions; and shall rejoice in

[q] Norris on Reason and Faith, p. 206, 207.
[r] *Tit.* i. 2.   [s] 1 *Tim.* iii. 15.   [t] *Heb.* xi. 10.
[u] 2 *Tim.* i. 12.   [w] 2 *Tim.* iii. 17.

every

every opportunity of making a publick confession of them with our mouths, testifying openly to others what we have inwardly felt and experienced ourselves.

As by Faith is meant, not only a general belief in Christ, but a confidential trust, a cordial acquiescence in his merits and mediation, as our Saviour and Redeemer; so by confession, in like manner, something more is to be understood, than a mere verbal acknowledgement of what he did and suffered for us. It is solemnly owning his mediatorial authority, and professing all gratitude and praise for the blessings and mercies secured for us by him, whose love was stronger than death: And though this confession with the mouth be not an efficient cause of holiness, it is not improperly reputed one of those necessary good works, flowing from the powerful energy of a true Faith. It is not mechanically repeating a form of words arranged into Creeds and Articles; but it is the visible testimony of a virtuous life, deriving its obedience from evangelical motives, which is the true available confession of Christ. And as this confession

sion must be thus illustrated in the practice and lives of men, so must it be publickly declared with their mouths; for to believe in Christ, and not to publish and glory in such belief, would be, like Nicodemus, to come to him secretly and in the dark; if not rather, like Peter, to renounce him in the hour of difficulty and temptation.

Whosoever, says our divine Master, *shall confess me before men*, openly acknowledging his fidelity to me, *him will I confess also before my Father which is in heaven*, rewarding him as solemnly as he hath owned me. *But whosoever shall deny*, renounce, or be ashamed of *me*, or his relation to me *before men, him will I also deny*, disown, and reject, in the most conspicuous manner, even *before my Father which is heaven, and before the angels of God* [x].

This declaration abundantly marks the necessity of an outward profession of the Gospel, as well as of the inward principle of Faith. Such a profession is necessary,

[x] *Matt.* x. 32, 33. *Luke* xii. 8, 9.

that

that men mistake not in a matter of so great consequence, but may *be ready always to give an answer to every one that asketh them a reason of the hope that is in them* [y] ; that they may be taught to avoid error and confusion, and may be early guarded against any destructive doctrines which, through ignorance or design, may occasionally begin anew to weaken the truths and evidences of the Gospel. Moreover that proper means of defence may be at hand, and comprised in such terms as may best express the precise meaning of the word of God; those leading articles which either comprehend the fundamentals of Christianity, distinguishing it in general from other Religions, or are the descriptive terms of Communion in the several Churches of Christ, have usually been drawn up under the mode or denomination of Creeds; and these are made the test of admission into the Christian Church in general, as well as into the profession of every religious community.

[y] 1 *Pet.* iii. 15.

Not that the Church takes upon herself indiscriminately to propose articles of Faith to be received and assented to, upon her own authority; but, upon the full persuasion and conviction of their being agreeable to the revealed will of God. The Apostles themselves judged this to be expedient, the better to deliver down to latest posterity, *according to the proportion* or analogy *of Faith* [z], pure and unadulterated that Doctrine which they preached. They plainly foresaw that heresies would, in after times, spring up and multiply, *and some would depart* or apostatize *from the Faith, by giving heed to seducing spirits* [a]. It was therefore the exhortation of St. Paul to his beloved Timothy, that he should *keep that which was committed to his trust* [b]: or, as he afterwards explains it, should *hold fast that form of sound words* [c]; that pattern or exemplar of divine truths, which he had deposited with him. So necessary did it seem to this great Apostle, to secure the assent of believers to

---

[z] *Rom.* xii. 6.   Κατα τλν αναλογιαν της πιστεως.
[a] 1 *Tim.* iv. 1.   Αποστησονται τινες της πιστεως.
[b] 1 *Tim.* vi. 20.   [c] 2 *Tim.* i. 13.

that

that system of doctrines which he had committed to the particular care of this his favourite convert, *his own son in the Faith*[d]; as containing necessary directions to him, and to all future pastors of the church, for the conscientious discharge of their duty, when advanced to stations of rule and government in the ministry.

This assent was originally required of the Catechumens, previous to their Baptism, from the very first institution of Christianity[e]. A profession of faith, a promise

---

[d] 1 *Tim.* i. 2.

[e] We read, *Acts*, ch. ii. that an open publick profession, or declaration of obedience to the Faith of *Jesus* as *Lord and Christ*, with *repentance of sins*, were the terms which St. Peter represented to those Jews, who were awakened, and converted by his first Sermon at Jerusalem upon the day of Pentecost, as indispensable requisites, before they could be received by the initiatory rites of Baptism into the Gospel-covenant. Thus when Philip *preached Jesus* to the Æthiopian Eunuch, whose conversion is recorded in *Acts*, ch. viii. *I believe that Jesus Christ is the Son of God*, was the confession he made previous to his admission into the Christian Church. Thus also, *Believe on the Lord Jesus Christ*, was the stipulated condition, when Paul and Silas baptized the Jailer at Philippi, *Acts*, ch. xvi. This was the apostolical usage. "The declaration "of Justin the Martyr, (in the next century, Apol. I. Sect. "79.) concerning Baptism, sheweth, how such as the Church "in those days did baptize, made profession of Christian be-"lief, and undertook to live accordingly." Hooker Eccles. Pol. B. v. S. 63.

of obedience, by way of solemn stipulation, was the prescriptive rule in all the churches. In the infancy indeed of the Gospel, when faith was strong, and errors were few, the form was short, and the words were simple: "The substance of Christian belief was compendiously drawn up into few and short articles, to the end that the weakness of no man's wit might either hinder altogether the knowledge, or excuse the utter ignorance of needful things[f]." Afterwards when men began to corrupt the simplicity of truth, preaching in effect *another Gospel, than that they had received*[g], and reproaching the Church, that its highest point of wisdom was implicit belief; and many erroneous notions were most industriously disseminated: It became necessary, not to propose new articles of Faith, for no Church upon earth is entrusted with such powers; but to ascertain the sense and import of those before established upon the foundation of scriptural and apostolical authority.

[f] Hooker's Ecclef. Polity. B. v. S. 18.
[g] *Gal.* i. 9.

In doing this, the Church doth not arrogate to herself the power of lording it over the conscience; but only to declare her sense and resolution of controverted points; to preserve peace and unity in her services; and to prevent dissensions and animosities amongst her members. Her determination however is of no farther weight, than as a probable argument for the right interpretation of Scripture; for after all, faith in fundamentals is the necessary undeniable obligation; and the Scriptures, as they are the only center of union between Christians, so are they the sole rule of Christ's Faith. " Now the prin-
" ciples whereupon we do build our souls,
" have their evidence where they had their
" original, and as received from thence
" we adore them, we hold them in reve-
" rend admiration, we neither argue nor
" dispute about them, we give unto them
" that assent which the Oracles of God re-
" quire. . . . That therefore which is true,
" and neither can be discerned by sense,
" nor concluded by mere natural princi-
" ples, must have principles of revealed
" truth

"truth whereupon to build itself, and an habit of faith in us wherewith principles of that kind are apprehended [h]."

As no Religion can be maintained or kept up without some system of belief; so no religious society can be established without some rule or badge of distinction, without some proof or evidence of the harmony of faith and confession received by that society. The Church of England, with a candour almost peculiar to herself, freely acknowledges, "that whatsoever is not read in Scripture, nor may be proved thereby, is not to be required of any man, that it should be believed as an article of the Faith, or be thought requisite or necessary to Salvation [i]." "That as the Church ought not to decree any thing against Holy Writ, so besides the same ought it not to enforce any thing to be believed for necessity of Salvation [k]." And those Creeds which she receives, she receives and professes upon the presumption, "that they may be proved by most certain

[h] Hooker's Eccles. Polity, B. v. S. 63.
[i] Art. VI.   [k] Art. XX.

"war-

"warrants of Holy Scripture [l]." Where this appeal fails, she is desirous that the authority which enjoins such doctrines, or interpretations of them, should fail also.

Under such liberal concessions and declarations, she hath adopted and inserted, in the publick services of her religious Offices, those formularies or confessions of Faith, "which were the Creeds of the "Western Church before the Reforma"tion; and because at the Reformation she "withdrew from nothing but what was "corrupt; and therefore these being Ca"tholick and sound, she still retains "them [m]." But however so cautious is she not arbitrarily to impose doctrines of Faith upon her members; that if we attend to the restrictions in those articles just now referred to, it will evidently appear, that these several Creeds are not received and recommended, either upon their own imaginary authority; or upon the credit of the reputed composers of them; but, upon the supposition that they are grounded upon the foundation of Scrip-

[l] Art. VIII.
[m] Wheatley's Moyers Lectures, Sermon II. p. 84.

ture,

ture, as perfectly confonant to the Doctrines delivered in those Sacred Writings; and as being little else, than so many allowed deduced extracts from them.

Upon this allegation, the Doctrines they contain have ever been held as truths of real moment and importance. As such they were at first compiled; as such they have ever since been maintained and defended; and as such the acknowledgement of them in every Christian Church hath been uniformly received, and they have been declared to be the Catholick Faith. The formal and precise terms indeed in which they are conceived, may not perhaps be found expressly or literally in so many words in Scripture; yet do they contain and affirm the same Doctrines which those divine Oracles of truth teach and express in other terms, or in words of the same import and signification. These we should have been as much obliged to receive and abide by, if they had not been modelled into the form of Creeds; because they are founded upon the revealed will of God: And the several articles which constitute them, are those very Doctrines, in the belief of which Christianity consists; and by which Christians must hereafter be examined and judged.

So careful is the Church to instruct and retain her members in that sound Faith which Christ and his Apostles left in charge as a sacred deposit; that as with the heart men are required to believe to justification, so with the mouth confession should be made of those articles, which the heart acknowledges as containing the substance of godly Faith. *Whosoever abideth not in the doctrine of Christ, hath not God*[n], nor any communion or interest with him. Creeds therefore are necessary barriers to prevent the inroads of those false teachers, who either from too violent an attachment to a favourite hypothesis, or, upon the presumption of the powers of natural Reason, take upon them to contradict, or explain away the peculiar doctrines of Revelation; such who privily *bring in*, or by various insinuations, *lying in wait to deceive*[o], are assiduous to introduce *damnable heresies*, here-

[n] 2 *John*, ver. 9.
[o] *Ephes.* iv. 14.

fies productive of calamitous and destructive consequences, which tend to the renouncing and *denying* the powers, grace, merits, satisfaction, and atonement of *the Lord that bought* and redeemed *them* [p]; even *the only Lord God, and our Lord Jesus Christ* [q].

This is the language of two Apostles, describing the nature of such heinous offences. Indeed the Scriptures throughout speak of the authors and fomenters of such pernicious Doctrines in terms of the severest indignation and abhorrence. They call them *ravening* and *grievous wolves* [r], *liars* [s], *deceivers* [t], *seducers* [u], *false prophets, yea Antichrists* [w]. But notwithstanding all these explicit marks of direct reprobation, the subtle adversary of God and man hath ever been incessant in *sowing tares amongst the wheat* [x]; and Heresy is a general calamity which hath more or less affected the universal Church, from the very foundation of Christianity: And though it may sometimes assume an harmless and indifferent meaning, yet in the religious acceptation

---

[p] 2 Pet. ii. 1.   [q] Jude, ver. 4.   [r] Matt. vii. 15.
Acts xx. 29.   [s] 1 John ii. 22.   [t] 2 John, ver. 7.
[u] 1 John ii. 26.   [w] 1 John iv. 1, and 3.   [x] Matt. xiii. 25.

of the word, it is for the most part understood in a bad sense, as implying error, that is, mistaking false Doctrines for true: For though every error be not an Heresy, yet falshood and error constitute the most usual idea of it. It is also an error in fundamentals, subversive of truth and piety; as in the instance before produced by St. Peter, of those who *denied the Lord who bought them*[y]: Which, whether it precisely means denying the reality of Christ's human or divine nature, or his satisfaction, is an error of the first magnitude; whether we refer it to the Nicolaitans and Gnosticks, those early disturbers of the peace of the Church; or, whether we apply it to the Arians and Socinians, the succeeding enemies of the Faith; or indeed by whatever respect men deny the Lord, their Redeemer, and their God, his nature, or his offices, it must be an heresy of perdition; such as distinguishes itself by its opposition to some of the main branches of the Gospel Faith, promotes discord and confusion; and by traducing the honour of his Son, is nothing less than blasphemy against God.

[y] 2 *Pet.* ii. 1.

There are indeed those who make Heresy and Schism, if not the same, yet as to their consequences very nearly allied: For though the weight and importance of the Doctrine denied be what principally impresses the signature of Heresy upon it; yet even an error, which is not fundamental, if it be obstinately adhered to, and openly published, leading to the breach of Charity and Peace, may not improperly deserve the name, and incur the same censure. When men rashly and wantonly adopt any singular, though not offensive, opinions in Religion, (and opinion is only something between ignorance and knowledge) yet if they sharply contend about them, persevere in, and propagate them to others, they give them in some degree the nature of heretical pravity.

Contentions are often as violent about smaller points, as greater matters. If by these means, different Sects are formed and encouraged upon principles of speculation and absolute indifference, we are authorized by St. Paul to give such dissensions the appellation of Schisms and Heresies. I *hear*,

hear, says this vigilant Apostle in one of his Epistles to the Corinthians, *that there be divisions or schisms among you* [z]. From thence ascending as to an higher degree of the same crime, he adds, *for there must be also heresies among you*, that the faith and steadiness of those *which are approved may be made manifest* [a]. Such differences in opinion, when applied to the breaking the peace and unity of the Church by needless and uncharitable disputes, bear the appellation of Schisms. If they increase and proceed so far as to subvert the Doctrines of Faith and Truth, they then become the aggravated crime of Heresy. And this is a kind of lust or wantonness of the mind, of so corrupt and vicious a complection, as to be ranked *among the works of the flesh* [b], proceeding from that natural corruption which *defiles the mind* [c]; for strife, seditions, wraths, envyings, and such like, are its usual concomitants.

Systematical Divines have indeed been too apt to consider Heresy in two lights,

[z] 1 *Cor*. xi. 18.   [a] 1 *Cor*. xi. 19.   [b] *Gal*. v. 19, 20. [c] *Tit*. i. 15.

SERMON VII. 201

as simple and compound. A distinction more nice than necessary; for it may possibly happen to be no more than mere opinion or theory; an intellectual error only, and so not cognizable by man; but solely under his jurisdiction who trieth and searcheth the heart. It is practical and doctrinal heresy against which the Church hath power to guard her members, to prevent, as much as in her lieth, the publication and infection of such error and falshood; and her censures are directed, not so much against simple opinions entertained in the mind, as against errors taught and scattered abroad [d].

Such are the false teachers we find described by some ancient writers, who in the name of Christ and Moses fight against them both [e]. Such are those, who scruple not to communicate with the Church, and perhaps subscribe to its Articles, and wait at its Altars; whilst, by their words and

[d] V. Forbesii Instructiones Hist. Theol. L. xiv. C. 1. de discrimine Ecclesiæ Catholicæ, et Hæreseos, et Schismatis.

[e] Επ ονοματι Χριϛȣ και Μωσεως, πολεμȣσι Χριϛω και Μωσει, και εν δορα αρροατων τ̄ λυκον κατακρυπτȣσιν. Constitutiones Apostolicæ, L. vi. Cap. 13.

writings, they are induſtriouſly ſullying the purity of its Faith, and calling in queſtion the truth of its doctrines; overlooking, deſpiſing, or rather inſenſible of the immorality of ſo baſe and wicked a conduct, from the preſumptuous confidence of the imaginary innocency of their error. Surely they who can ſo eaſily ſatisfy themſelves, had need to examine well the force of thoſe arguments from whence ſuch concluſions are drawn: What they may deem to be merely notional, or ſimply ſpeculative principles, and too indifferent to have any influence upon practice, may perhaps prove to be eſſential, fundamental Doctrines, and the belief of them neceſſary to entitle them to partake of the benefits of Chriſtianity. St. Peter and St. Paul, in direct contradiction of this fancied abſolute innocence of error, ſtrongly maintain the criminality of thoſe, who, without acting contrary to the convictions of their minds, neglect, (where means of information may be had) a proper impartial care in forming their principles of action [f]. St. Peter in a paſ-

---

[f] See *Acts* iii. 17. 1 *Tim.* i. 13.

ſage

sage before referred to, very particularly acquaints us with the common methods which these deceivers make use of to introduce their Doctrines. *They privily*, says he, *bring in damnable heresies*[g]; privily, that is, under colour of truth and piety, and a sincere regard for the honour of the Gospel; not declaring at once their real sentiments, but slyly and artfully; the word in its original meaning is strongly expressive of the craft and subtle insinuation of such reprobate teachers.

If the apostolical age itself felt the pernicious effects of a vain, dogmatizing spirit; if succeeding periods of the Church have experienced the same inconveniences; we are not to expect the present days to be more exempt from such troubles, and such complaints; in which so *many unruly, and vain talkers, and deceivers*[h] abound. We have seen what our own Church hath done to preserve the rule

[g] 2 Pet. ii. 1. Οιτινες παρεισαξυσιν αιρεσεις απωλειας.
[h] Tit. i. 10.

of Faith, as delivered in Scripture, pure and uncorrupt, in order to check the progress of heretical invaders; that none of her members be seduced for want of proper caution or previous instruction: *That we may all speak the same thing, and that there be no divisions among us; but that we be perfectly joined together in the same mind, and in the same judgement* [i].

What her doctrinal principles are, does evidently appear from those Creeds she hath embodied in her publick religious services, as so many scriptural truths. Notwithstanding all the many popular and plausible objections which are so frequently and so invidiously alleged against these Creeds, this is certain, that none but those who are enemies to the Faith of Christ, will ever oppose the Doctrines established in them. For this reason it is expedient, and even necessary, to retain these criterions of sound Doctrine. " And when we have no ene-
" mies remaining to find fault with the
" Doctrines, there will be none to object

[i] 1 *Cor.* i. 10.

" against

"against the use of the Creeds, or so much as to wish to have them laid aside [k]." For the same authority which affirmeth that *with the heart, man believeth unto Righteousness*; declareth also, that *with the mouth confession is made unto Salvation.*

[k] Dr. Waterland's Critical History of the Athanasian Creed, p. 292.

SERMON VIII.

HEB. IV. 2.

Unto us was the Gospel preached, as well as unto them, but the word preached did not profit them, not being mixed with faith in them that heard it.

WHEN we attentively consider those several evidences, which abundantly demonstrate the Gospel of of Christ to be the word of God; some of which it hath been the endeavour of the preceding Discourses to illustrate: It cannot but afford us frequent occasions of wonder

wonder and concern to obferve, that its acknowledged truth and importance are not always accompanied with a proportionable degree of weight and influence on the lives of men; and that, however excellent its doctrines, however ftrong the motives, or forcible the obligations contained in it are, for promoting virtue and knowledge, yet neverthelefs they are too often found infufficient or ineffectual to regulate the general practice of the world.

Hence wicked men and unbelievers have advanced a popular objection againft the truth and authority of Chriftianity, by arguing, that fuch a fcheme of Salvation can hardly be fuppofed to be the revealed will of the Almighty, from the little efficacy it is feen to have even upon profeffed believers. They hear them fpecioufly haranguing upon all the feveral branches and peculiar characters of their Religion, yet without giving that teftimony of their conviction, and of their faith, which their Mafter hath declared to be the only infallible fign of both, their love to God and man.

It

SERMON VIII.

It were to be wished indeed, for the honour of Religion itself, that this objection could be answered by denying the fact, rather than by seeking after reasons to account for the misconduct. But whatever be the cause, it is certainly not owing to any defect in the Gospel itself; either for want of more light, or clearer instruction: For surely, it hath all the external and internal proofs of truth which the most profound enquiry can demand; and it affords also all the most reasonable conviction that an intelligent and free agent can desire.

What kind or degree of influence then could satisfy such objectors, unless they expected that God should make men mere machines, and compel them to be good, whether they would or no? He has supported his word however with as engaging, persuasive, and powerful motives, as are consistent with our freedom of will, and moral agency, so far to direct our obedience, as to render us responsible for our deviations from it.

SERMON VIII.

In the foregoing part of this Epistle, the Apostle expatiates upon the singular excellency of that Gospel he was recommending to his Hebrew converts, as greatly superior to *the word spoken by Angels*[a]. Such and so great was the original pre-eminence of Christ, that those glorious Beings, who were honourably distinguished at the delivery of the Law, at the promulgation of the Covenant made with the Fathers at mount Sinai, were only so many *ministring spirits sent forth* [b] to attend him upon earth, and to act in subserviency to his orders: For exalted as their nature was, it was greatly subordinate to his transcendent character, who *inherited a more excellent name than they*[c], as being the Son of God himself. The Jews had ever been accustomed to entertain the profoundest veneration for Moses their divine Legislator: He truly, *was faithful in all his house*[d]; but it was only *as a servant,* in an inferior department, appointed *for a testimony of those things which were to be spoken after*[e], of that better dispensation which the Apostle

[a] *Heb.* ii. 2. [b] *Heb.* i. 14. [c] *Heb.* i. 4.
[d] *Heb.* iii. 2. [e] *Heb.* iii. 5.

was

was now announcing. If they had examined the promises of God made to Adam, to Abraham, and to others of their ancestors recorded in the Law and the Prophets, they would have found comprised in them the sum and substance of that doctrine which *he preached* unto them: The whole Mosaical administration being calculated to confirm this word, and previously to instruct them in the nature and meaning, and prepare them for the accomplishment of those promises, *until the time of* full and final *Reformation should come*ᶠ; when *that dispensation* should be revealed, in which *God would gather together in one all things in Christ*ᵍ, and their religious worship and services should be directed to their proper spiritual designation.

Upon this account *it was necessary that the word of God should first have been spoken to them*ʰ; and they were informed that the present more perfect manifestation of it, by the personal appearance and preaching of Jesus or Christ the Messiah, was in

ᶠ *Heb.* ix. 10. ᵍ *Ephes.* i. 10.
ʰ *Acts* xiii. 46.

truth nothing more than the carrying on and compleating of the same original plan of Revelation, which had been previously communicated to them through the medium of their own Scriptures. From hence arose the equal obligation of faith and obedience to Christ in Jew as well as in Christian. But with all these extraordinary signatures of divine Authority, the Apostle observes, that *the word preached,* or of hearing, as it is more literally rendered[i], actually profited them not; that is, they received no advantage from, they did not improve it, though it was the foundation of their own Religion; because it was *not mixed with faith in them that heard it.* Agreeably to what we are told elsewhere, that *faith cometh by hearing, and hearing by the word of God*[k] declaring the necessity of it. This is the Doctrine meant to be enforced in the passage before us; that as *the word* of God *preached* formerly to the Fathers *in the wilderness,* became unfruitful to them *because of* their disobedience and *unbelief*[l]; so neither will it profit us Christians to have *the*

[i] O λογος της ακοης.
[k] *Rom.* x. 17.   [l] *Heb.* iii. 17. 19.

Gospel

SERMON VIII.

Gospel preached, and to hear and read those Scriptures which reveal it, unless we receive and obey it as the word of God. This will appear more plainly if we consider,

 First, The connexion between the Word and Faith.

 Secondly, The causes which obstruct their united Influence.

The union between the Word and Faith is so close and intimate, that as Faith cannot be without the Word, so the Word without or separate from the other, is nothing more than a dead letter, or mere useless Creed. Not that the efficacy of the Word in the least dependeth upon us, for that standeth sure and immutable: *For what if some did not believe? shall their unbelief* or rejection of the Gospel, as St. Paul argues with the Romans, *make the faith,* or promises *of God* void and *without effect*[m]? *God forbid,* that such a thought should be harboured; *yea* surely, *let God be true, but*

[m] *Rom.* iii. 3.

every man, who indulgeth such blasphemous cogitations, *a lyar*ⁿ. His promises are made to faithful servants: *If we believe not, yet he abideth faithful; he cannot deny himself*°, or frustrate all his solemn declarations of pardon and acceptance.

This word of God is moreover expressly noted to be *quick and powerful, and exceeding sharp*ᵖ; but still it cannot penetrate into the heart except Faith shall first procure its admission; and it will not be *the power* or instrument *of God unto Salvation*, but *to those who believe. Therein* indeed *is the Righteousness of God revealed from faith to faith*ᵠ, by fresh, repeated, and increasing exercises of it; which, in the progress of our religious attainments, will be ever opening to us farther and more encouraging views of the inexhaustible grace and fulness of that glorified head of our nature, who *came that we might have life, and that we might have it more abundantly*ʳ. For we must first believe the Word, before we can accept or partake of the blessings of it: Then shall

ⁿ *Rom.* iii. 4.   ° 2 *Tim.* ii. 13.   ᵖ *Heb.* iv. 12.
ᵠ *Rom.* i. 16, 17.   ʳ *John* x. 10.

we

we be empowered *to set to our seal, that God is true*[s]; and his justification will appear the same in every different period of the life of grace. Not that the word is, at any time, less powerful, or less able to convince or convert us; but the promise is only to believers: And as there can be no Faith, where there are no Scriptures, or revealed will of God to enjoin and prove it, so Faith is the life and spirit of the Word, according to that saying of the Prophet, *the just shall live by Faith*[t]; *without which it is impossile to please God*[v]. Indeed wherever the Gospel is truly received, it never fails of its full successful efficacy in promoting the interests of Virtue and Religion. But when any are contented to remain in an unconverted sinful state, they may be confidently pronounced to all good purposes, unbelievers or rejectors of the Word.

Such was the power of God, such was the operative prevalency of preaching at the beginning, that numbers were con-

[s] *John* iii. 33. [t] *Hab.* ii. 4.
[v] *Heb.* xi. 6.

verted at once to the Christian Faith. Such also of a sudden was the prodigious change of their conduct from sin unto holiness, that they became as *new creatures*[u]: Nay, so astonishing was their renovation, that they who had experienced it themselves, and therefore could best describe it, represent it as similar in its effects, and as strange in its operations, as if it had been *a passing from death unto life*[w]: They call it *a rising from the dead*[x]; *a putting on the new man*[y]; *a burial with Christ in baptism, wherein also we are risen with him through the faith of the operation* or energy *of God*[z].

This extraordinary effect of evangelical Faith lasted not only during the fervour of apostolical instruction and example, but continued some ages after in the Church; insomuch that ancient ecclesiastical writers observe, that when Christians were apprehended and brought before magistrates to answer for themselves, none were found to come under the denomination of criminals:

---

[u] 2 *Cor.* v. 17. [w] 1 *John* iii. 14. [x] *Ephes.* v. 14.
[y] *Ephes.* iv. 24.
[z] *Col.* ii. 12. Διὰ τῆς πίστεως τῆς ἐνεργείας τȣ Θεȣ.

None

None of them was charged with or proved guilty of a breach of the moral law. No other accusation being alleged against any, but that of a steady adherence to the Religion of Christ [b].

Certainly this is an undeniable proof of the power of the Gospel in those primitive times; and undoubtedly it would have the same good effect upon us, in these later days, if we believed it as firmly, and upon the same principles as they did. Nay, there never was a time, since the name of *Jesus* was first preached, even in the darkest and most ignorant ages of the Church, but the minds of believers were more or less affected, according to the sincerity and simplicity of their faith. And if we should compare the Christian nations of the pre-

---

[b] This is the great complaint which the ancient apologists and historians are ever making, that the name of Christian alone, without any other supposed or imputed crime, was a sufficient charge for conviction and execution. These are Christians, was a mark of ignominy frequently inscribed upon a tablet denoting their guilt, and carried before them, when the martyrs were exposed to the fury and derision of a crouded amphitheatre. See Justin Martyr's Apol. S. 3. and 32. Tertullian's Apol. c. 3. and 45. Euseb. Ecclef. Hist. L. iv. c. 19. and L. v. c. 1.

sent age, with those heathens who are unacquainted with the Gospel, we shall soon be convinced of the amazing difference there is between the knowledge of the Christian faith, and the ignorance of it.

Far be it therefore from us to suppose gospel motives to Godliness any ways weak or ineffectual, because some wicked or unthinking persons may go under the appellation of Christians, upon whom they may seem to have little or no influence; since there is ample proof of many (very many) whose general tenor of life demonstrates, how greatly they are persuaded of the grace and truth of Christ; *whom having not seen, they love*[c].

Surely, none of us are such poor proficients in Virtue and Religion, as not to be able confidently to appeal to our own consciences, whether the voice of God, and the secret whispers of the holy spirit of Grace have not frequently prevented our falling into sin; or, if we have yielded to

[c] 1 *Pet.* i. 8.

the temptations of it, as frequently awakened and urged us to repentance? And whether they have not afterwards given us the reviving comfortable assurances that our iniquities are pardoned, and the guilt of them washed away *by the sprinkling of the blood of Jesus Christ*[d], *who hath obtained eternal Redemption for us*[e]? Neither can there be a doubt, but that the power and conviction of Faith strengthens and preserves us from sin, and invigorates us with the most animating persuasions of the blessings of the Gospel, *through the knowledge of God, and of Jesus our Lord*[f]. *To as many as* thus *receive him doth Christ give power to become the Sons of God, even to them that believe on his name*[g]. So manifest is the connexion between the Word and Faith.

Secondly, We will now consider the causes which obstruct their influence. The first and general reason is that which is hinted in the text, the want of a due proportion of faith, or a strong and leading inclination to unbelief, which in the pre-

---

[d] 1 *Pet.* i. 2. [e] *Heb.* ix. 12. [f] 2 *Pet.* i. 2.
[g] *John* i. 12.

ceding chapter is called *an evil heart of unbelief*[h]. The *Word*, or Gospel *preached* as naturally produceth faith, as the cause does the effect; but not being properly *mixed* or incorporated together, they fail of the necessary beneficial consequences. Not that the Gospel is either absolutely rejected or any ways lightly spoken of; but because the meaning or import of faith itself is greatly mistaken; and something very different from it usurps the name, and is deemed the essence and substance, and contended for as earnestly as if it was the grace itself.

Faith, in the evangelical sense of the word, doth not signify an opinion taken up at random, or from authority, but a fixed, steady persuasion both of the truth and certainty of the things believed, and of their great weight and importance. *Because iniquity abounds, the love of many is waxed cold*[i]; and numbers take their Religion upon trust, without examining into the nature and foundation of it. *Giving* no *earnest heed to the*

[h] *Heb.* iii. 12.
[i] *Matt.* xxiv. 12.

things

SERMON VIII.

things which they have heard, they easily *let them slip*[k]. They see nothing divine and admirable in it, nothing so effectual and persuasive as to prevail upon them to answer the injunctions of it. They receive indeed and profess it, but as a thing of course, and without due attention how much their welfare or their ruin depends upon their feeling the power and living the life of Faith; or, on the contrary, yielding to the suggestions of negligence and incredulity.

But it is not a superficial assent, which the Scriptures inculcate as that Faith, the fruits whereof will bring Salvation. This is nothing more than a blind opinion; such a mere formal Faith as cannot supply us with sufficient powers to restrain the violence of the passions, or correct the desires of the will. Indeed this sort of counterfeit Faith doth very often exert itself for the name and sound of Religion, and exults in its eagerness and animosity in exposing the imaginary sin and folly of a different judgement with regard to religious

[k] *Heb.* ii. 1.

princi-

principles. When this active zeal shall impel men to expressions of rancour and bitterness, or to actions of violence and persecution, we have too much cause to suspect that they are more solicitous for victory than for truth. The spirit of the Gospel is love, gentleness, and humility. Where these are wanting, whatever pretensions we may make to truth and faith, they will be but so many vain and clamorous appeals; because their necessary concomitants, those good fruits of the Spirit, are not found in them.

Another hindrance detrimental to the salutary influence of Gospel Faith is, when men mistake the shadow for the substance, and suppose Religion to be what it is not: Making it to consist as much in an attention to prescribed formalities, as in the exercises of inward piety. This is connected with, and is the natural consequence of the former obstacle. In this case the Gospel motives, though they may be embraced and believed, will only excite to outward duties, or shews of godliness, and not in the least contribute to forward that essential change of the heart and affections, which

which is the only perfection of true Religion, the only solid assurance of a justifying Faith. By the rigid and punctual observance of ritual injunctions, an habitual facility of ostentatious, deceitful Religion may be acquired, without knowing what is meant by the inward powers of it.

Thus the Jews of old were frequently censured by our blessed Lord for their scrupulous adherence to the traditions of their Fathers; their tenacious observation of external rites and services too often leading them to neglect the weightier matters of the Law, the moral commandments of God. Christians likewise may love the word, and flatter themselves their faith is perfectly pure and sound, because they walk in all the appointed ordinances of the Church, and earnestly press uniformity to her laws upon principles of Necessity and Salvation; whilst it is to be feared, the bare profession of believing is but too frequently mistaken for the inward act of Faith: For the Religion of a Christian doth not consist so much in fine notions, or orthodox opinions, as in the cultivation

of

of those several virtues and graces which adorn the mind, which set forth the glory of God, and promote the general good of mandkind. We Christians, says one of the ancients, do not speak great things, but we live them [1]. They did nothing for opinion, but every thing for conscience sake; remembring that *the end of the commandment is charity, out of a pure heart, and of a good conscience, and of faith unfeigned* [m].

To these reasons which render the Word and Faith ineffectual and unprofitable, others of a more vitiated nature may be added. Such as an inattention to the doctrines of Religion in general, when they are never made the subject of thought and reflection. Motives are only so far effectual, as they are applied to the mind: If they are not weighed and considered, they are of no avail; like so many idle and unmeaning words, they vanish in sound, carrying nothing on to perfection.

---

[1] *Non magna eloquimur, sed vivimus.* Min. Fœlix.—— *Nihil opinionis gratia, omnia conscientiæ faciam;* is the saying of another ancient worthy. [m] 1 Tim. i. 5.

Next

Next to this, is that over anxious folicitude for temporal advantages, which so engrosses the time and thoughts of many, that they have no leisure or opportunity duly to attend to the superior excellencies of a divine and spiritual Faith. The seed of the Gospel, though ever so good, sown upon such a soil is *choked with cares, and riches, and pleasures of this life, and brings no fruit to perfection* [n]. Men thus attached to the good things of this world, and absorbed in the splendid pageantries of it, lose all taste and relish of the joys and comforts of Religion, which are only *spiritually discerned* [o], and with the eye of Faith.

To such the *Gospel is hid*, but *it is hid to them* because they *are lost* [p]. It is not for want of a more perfect Revelation: It is not that the Doctrines of it are obscure and unintelligible: It is not that the Apostles and Evangelists *handled the word of God deceitfully*, concealing or disguising any part of it. Far from it, with the utmost per-

[n] *Luke* viii. 14.
[o] 1 *Cor.* ii. 14.
[p] 2 *Cor.* iv. 3.

spicuity

spicuity and plainness, *by manifestation of the truth*[q], they made it perfectly clear and visible. The darkness and the ignorance which the Apostles complained of, originated from the malice of *the God of this world, who hath blinded the minds of them which believe not*[r], in such a manner, *that they hate the light, neither come to the light, lest their deeds should be reproved*[s]: For the knowledge of the truth discovers to them, what they are unwilling to see, the base servitude of sin, and what they are more unwilling to acknowledge, the danger of their sinful state. Whilst they reflect, so long are they miserable: Whilst the Gospel reasons with them *of righteousness, temperance, and judgement to come*, they wish with *Felix*, to put off so ungrateful a subject *to a* more *convenient season*[t]. Their passions and their prejudices so overcome them, that they are deaf to all the advice, and blind to all the motives of the Gospel, so that the knowledge of it profits them not. Certainly as the love of God is so conspicuous in his offers of grace and par-

[q] 2 *Cor.* iv. 2.   [r] 2 *Cor.* iv. 4.   [s] *John* iii. 20.
[t] *Acts* xxiv. 25.

don,

SERMON VIII. 227

don, their state must be deplorable, who, through wilfulness pervert, through pride despise, or through carelessness neglect them, and thereby unhappily deprive themselves of the benefit thus graciously intended for them. Their only refuge from guilt must be their ignorance of their duty; which ignorance proceeds from their unwillingness to be at the pains to enquire after and to understand the conditions of it; when perhaps they are deficient in no other branch of knowledge, but that which alone *is able to make them wise unto Salvation* [u].

Upon these accounts, it is no wonder, that the evidences of the Word, and the persuasive convictions of Faith are not accompanied with better, and more desireable effects. Considering all things however, it is an abundant proof of their real excellency, that their success and prevalency are so great in the midst of such variety of sects, and of different religious denominations, whose divided, separate interests and principles are continually clashing with

[u] 2 *Tim.* iii. 15.

each other; by which unhappy divisions no small discredit is brought on the honour of Religion in general.

For how can we reasonably expect that the pure and peaceable temper of the Gospel should reside in a turbulent, intolerant, or persecuting disposition? How can Christianity be esteemed by those who are so devoted to the idol of their own proud reason, as to slight and scornfully to reject the aids of Grace and Revelation, and to question the credibility of those Doctrines which their own feeble powers cannot comprehend? How amazingly do greatness, wealth, and power engage the heart, and indispose it for attention to spiritual truths? How likewise can the arguments of Religion influence ignorant and vicious minds, who have neither time, nor abilities, nor inclination to reflect upon the necessity, obligation, or importance of them.

With so many obstructions to retard its progress, the little sway which Religion hath over the world is easily accounted for. Surrounded with innumerable soliciting tempta-

temptations, seduced by the example of a *faithless and perverse generation*ʷ; we may ask, *who* is it that *hath warned us to flee from the wrath to come*ˣ? Who is it that at any time disposeth us to holy duties, to virtuous actions, and inspireth us with good desires? Certainly no inherent natural power of our own, no arguments or persuasions of men, but the voice and word of God. It is the sound of this trumpet which awakens us from the death of Sin unto the life of Righteousness. It is this divine call of the Spirit which produceth in us a lively faith in Christ, and a filial obedience to his will. Without this, the wisest instructions of the best of men will be ineffectual.

If the word of God be fruitless, how much more so will be the word of men? If the Scriptures be not hearkened to, which are at hand, and whose divine Authority is acknowledged, it is impossible to hope, that under the dominion of a variety of prejudices, the words of weak and fal-

---
ʷ *Matt.* xvii. 17.
ˣ *Matt.* iii. 7.

lible men should meet with a favourable reception. But God hath promised to bestow a blessing upon his good seed, when sown upon a proper, kindly soil; so that by due cultivation it will spring up, and bring forth good fruit plentifully, even *unto life eternal*[y].

Such was the salutary and blessed effect which attended the first preachers of the Gospel; *the Lord working with them, and confirming the word with signs following*[z]. And when the miraculous power of his Grace, in the conversion of sinners, had once spread the alarm: *Sirs, what must I do to be saved*[a]? was the natural result of the awakened impression: They who were thus moved, *gladly received the word*[b]; *and believing, they rejoiced with joy unspeakable, and full of glory*[c]: The Spirit of God giving this zeal and earnestness to as many as were willing to embrace the offers of Gospel Love. Some indeed were deaf to the call, and believed not: But, shall their unbelief be alleged to exculpate others, who, after

[y] *John* iv. 36. [z] *Mark* xvi. 20. [a] *Acts* xvi. 30.
[b] *Acts* ii. 41. [c] 1 *Pet.* i. 8.

their

their example, flight all the importunate and affectionate addresses which God is ever making to them? Such must endure the dreadful consequences of their obstinacy and infidelity. God hath supported his Word and his Faith with a notoriety of evidence sufficient to satisfy every rational enquirer. If these accumulated proofs persuade not, nothing can. God hath provided no remedy for those who refuse to listen to such indisputable testimonies of his will and authority. They must perish through their own gainsaying and reprobate heart.

So long as there remain men of this disposition in the world, and such there ever will be, so long will the Cross of Christ be maligned. Fresh adversaries will be perpetually springing up, well trained and exercised in all the arts of sophistry and deceit. Ancient and exploded objections will be from time to time revived; and the most plausible appearances of truth and beauty will be employed in decorating anew the most offensive opinions. Many indeed and various are the disguises, and specious the fallacious coverings to elude detection: For error seldom shews itself in its own natural deformity, and the more subtle the poison, the infection is always the more malignant and fatal.

Such will ever be the case, when the pride of human understanding shall induce men to trust wholly to the strength of their own reason. This presumption deceived the philosophers of old. This faint glimmering light, in like manner, leads modern theorists into the mazes of error and mistake; when the foolishness of man undertakes to solve the mysteries of God, and leaves them to stand or fall by the decision of that deceitful balance. Hence is it, that many who pretend a veneration for the honour of God and Religion, shall yet accustom themselves to insult the person, and to traduce the Gospel of his Son; by reducing the former to the state of a mere man, and esteeming the latter as nothing more than a republication of the Law of Nature. Such reasoners are not disposed to receive even the plainest truths: They can see no necessity for any Saviour, but

but what their own imperfect virtue, or ideal sincerity can procure; nor any more preferable excellency in the precepts of the Christian, than in the dictates of natural Religion.

This is sacrificing to the idols of a miserably deluded imagination. They who can thus divert themselves with the incense of their own perfumes, may not a little exult in those applauses which the strangers to Revelation too inconsiderately bestow upon them.

Happily however they have not, they cannot succeed in their vanities: The *wisdom* of God, how boldly soever impeached, hath been fully *justified* by the zeal and vigilance *of her children*[a]: Whilst these seats of useful and ingenuous learning remain; so long, may we pronounce, the Gospel will be opposed in vain. The blessing of God hath so highly favoured these *schools of the Prophets*, that from thence have gone forth from time to time the ablest champions

[a] *Matt.* ii. 9.

and

and guardians of *the faith which was once delivered to the faints*[e]; whose natural and acquired abilities, improved by the knowledge of God, and sanctified by his grace, have been nobly exerted in so meritorious a cause, and enabled them to detect the folly and imposture of that *wisdom which descendeth not from above,* and to prove it to be *earthly, sensual, devilish*[f].

We need not refer to the labours of former days: We can with pleasure easily recollect and chearfully boast of a race of present worthies, not inferior to the generations that are past, who, with an inexhaustible fund of literature, and with equal sanctity of life and manners, have eminently distinguished themselves as well in defence of Revelation in general, as of particular branches of it: Who have elucidated scriptural difficulties and obscurities; have with precision and accuracy marked the progressive stages of Prophecies already accomplished, as well as pointed out those that are successively receiving their accomplishment; have

[e] *Jude,* ver. 3.
[f] *James* iii. 15.

evinced

evinced the nature, importance, and credibility of those miracles recorded in Scripture, which were the obvious and popular demonstrations of a divine agency; and have vindicated the scriptural Doctrine of the Trinity, and the honour, divinity, and personality of their Redeemer, and of the Holy Ghost, from the exceptions of those who have called them in question, with an arrogance and malignity peculiarly their own.

It were endless to enumerate the long list of those who have done honour to themselves, and have reflected credit on the places of their education, by taking an active part in favour of the Gospel of Christ, whenever *the way of truth* hath appeared to *be evil spoken of*[s], or insulted. The extensive knowledge, the sound judgement, and the manly rational criticism displayed upon such occasions ought at least to satisfy the objectors to it, that Christianity is not that irrational unnecessary system they would wish to have it repre-

[s] *2 Pet.* ii. 2.

sented;

sented; but that it is built upon the solid and irrefragable foundation of Reason and Argument, and is worthy their most deliberate attention. Would they but once allow themselves maturely to consider, and impartially to examine the strength of the evidences adduced in support of the truths of the Gospel; they would soon discover the weakness of those attempts which its adversaries have pertinaciously made to undermine and subvert it; and how greatly an obedient, reverential regard to its precepts would contribute to the happiness of mankind. Awakened by these impressions, they would proceed from strength to strength; would feel the happy effects of increasing light and conviction; would acknowledge the excellency, wisdom, and necessity of Revelation; and how much it is their duty and their interest seriously to reflect upon the rise and foundation of those principles, which have hitherto separated them from the knowledge and love of God in Christ; and of what importance it is that they should no longer continue to cherish in themselves, or encourage in others *an evil heart of unbelief*[h]. By pursuing these enquiries in the spirit of humility and devotion, they would become well qualified, from their own experience, and would rejoice to testify, with what singular truth and propriety the apostolical inference in the language of the text may be applied to unbelievers in general, that *the word preached did not profit them, not being mixed with faith in them that heart it.*

[h] *Heb.* iii. 12.

F I N I S.

www.ingramcontent.com/pod-product-compliance
Lightning Source LLC
Chambersburg PA
CBHW021405230426
43666CB00006B/647